# The Sooner You Know, The Better

Dear Teens & Twentysomethings,
It's Time to Fully Face Your Fears About
The Future and Embrace Who You Are

Sincerely Your Friend,

*Livi Redden*

To my mom for being my guardian angel
my dad for teaching me to finish strong
my sister for her constant encouragement
my ancestors & God for their solace

# CONTENTS

## PART 3. Doing

Pssttt . . . Hey. Real quick. This is Livi.

Do NOT skip the introduction. You need it for context. Otherwise this book will be like watching Endgame having never watched a single Marvel movie, not listening to a new album top to bottom, or putting the milk in before the cereal. All serious crimes against humanity in my book. You're not a criminal . . . are you? Okay then. Don't skip my introduction.

You can skip another person's introduction, but not mine.

# Introduction

---

# My "Why" and What to Expect

**Y**ou've probably opened this book because you're navigating, or at least trying to navigate, your teen or twentysomething years right now. You're trying to make sense of this weird, uncomfortable phase that some call emerging adulthood.

I'm in the same boat, my friend. As exciting and fun as this time of our lives is, this shit is no walk in the park. You've probably recently laid in your bed at night overwhelmed with the stress of trying to figure out your next step in life. You've probably recently left a family or social gathering a little irritated or overwhelmed by all the questions about "What's your plan?," "Are you dating anyone?," "Where are my grandbabies?," "How do you make money doing that?"

On top of that, I'd bet you've had some fear in the last few months about not making enough money to make ends meet, or your grades dropping from some impossible midterm, or not feeling ready to commit to your current relationship. I'd bet you've recently had feelings of deep, aching sadness about losing friends, or dealing with a crappy home life, or trying to recover from childhood trauma, or feeling like you just aren't good enough. If any of those things relate to you, I want you to take a deep breath. Give yourself a moment to be proud of yourself. Just one moment. You're doing the best you possibly can with the cards you've been dealt. You're learning. You're growing. You're a good person. And that's all we can ask of ourselves. Life isn't easy, and you're persevering anyway. That is something to celebrate and I mean that with deep sincerity. I feel so grateful that the world gets to experience the light that radiates from you. We need you. Cheesy, I know, but I don't care. That's a *big* reason why I wrote this book: to tell you that we really do need you. The real you. The you who's actually you.

This book will aid in your ability to harness and radiate the pieces of light and potential that may be lying dormant inside you. This book is not a step-by-step manual for your life; this book is a conversation starter. A conversation I feel could completely shift, for the better, the way society functions. That conversation is about the importance of understanding our minds, developing mindfulness, and improving emotional intelligence (EQ) sooner rather than later. If we can understand the importance of these concepts and develop these parts of ourselves right now as young people, it will free us to be ourselves. To be aligned and at peace. To live a good life. To navigate this rocky area of our lives with much more clarity. Sounds nice, right?

## My "Why"

So, who am I? Who's on the other side of this conversation you're having? Right now, I'm coming to you from my favorite table in my favorite coffee shop in San Diego. I'm drinking an iced chai alongside an overcooked slice of quiche.

It's seventy degrees outside, and I feel an abundance of love in my heart today. As the writer of a personal development book, I feel I'm supposed to act all chill and professional like a wise, straight-faced authority figure with a Ph.D. that has the answers you've waited your entire life to hear.

But that's not me. So, in the spirit of authenticity I just have to say—I'm so excited this book is in your hands! I'm excited we're embarking in this conversation together! Two homies ( maybe you're drinking an iced chai, too) talking about the roller coaster that is our teen and twentysomething years. I didn't write this book because I have the traditional credentials to do so. I wrote it because I believe in the sublime essence of people. I believe that I am intrinsically sublime, and I believe you are intrinsically sublime. The definition of sublime is ingrained into my mind: "to be of such beauty, excellence or grandeur as to inspire great awe or admiration." That's you, and that's me.

Why do I believe that? Because I've felt, to some degree, that sublime energy, that power, that potential in myself and in everyone that I have ever met. Everyone. I've felt that powerful energy in others and myself since I was young. As I grew up, I realized that not everyone felt that way about themselves. They didn't see what I saw. Beauty. Excellence. Grandeur. To me, that was the biggest tragedy. In so many people that light lies dormant for years, begging for release. Sometimes all people need is for someone to finally tell them how powerful they are—just one person to aid in unlocking that potential. It's devastating when I see lost potential, or someone's truest self disintegrate into nothingness. It sucks because like I said, we need you. Every light on this earth matters. It freaking matters.

A conversation starts with questions. This book was created because I went on a hunt to answer quite a few questions.

## Questions Worth Asking

Why aren't more people teaching teens and twentysomethings how to become more mindful and self-aware right now, *before* many big decisions are made in our teens & twenties? Why are we not teaching emotional intelligence in schools and to young adults? Why are we telling young people that they'll "just figure it out" when concepts that can provide 99 percent more clarity can be taught?

At this age, we're often brushed past and dismissed as being young and dumb. That's just the way it is and we can't change that about ourselves. This makes no sense. If there is a time to start understanding who you are, how you interact with the world, what you look for in relationships, how to cope with past trauma, and how to make more intentional decisions, it is 100 percent as a young person.

In my years of studying healing, psychology, mindset, neuroscience, sociology, mindfulness, the art of personal growth, I've rarely heard thought leaders in this space specifically targeting emerging adults (ages eighteen to twenty-five) with these concepts even though we need to know these concepts the most. The fact is many of life's most important decisions are often made in your twenties—determining a field of study or career, weighing marriage, deciding where to live, handling money, raising children, and many others with life-long impacts. That's why self-development, developed emotional intelligence, and increased mindfulness is best if we can start *now*. These big decisions don't have to be such scary big things. All we need is a little more intention and clarity to build a sturdier foundation in our teens and twenties to help set us up for a more intentionally and healthily created life in the future.

This book is an urgent alarm for my fellow emerging adults to intentionally enter a growth process *now* to make their lives easier later. (Side note: we'll all make some decisions that will result in less than ideal outcomes, which is also a part of the growing process, so the goal is not perfection).

Growing up, my challenging home life, which I'll expound on more later, jump-started my exposure to three topics—mindset, mindfulness, and EQ—at twelve years old. I had to have very real conversations with my family about death, hope, communication, empathy, honesty, forgiveness, sacrifice, healing, therapy, grief, sadness; tough conversations that are relatively unusual for an eleven or twelve-year-old to have. That being said, I feel so blessed that I lived in a home that openly spoke about these concepts and feelings. As I've grown older (I'm now in my twenties), I've found that many people aren't getting this jump-start or being exposed to these concepts until much later in life. As people, we often wait for disaster to strike before we become conscious enough to say to ourselves, *maybe I should change the way I live or think*, or *I should probably heal from my childhood trauma because it's resurfacing*, or *I'm not happy or fulfilled and something needs to change.*

Generally speaking, this consciousness doesn't hit until about halfway through life, where disaster often tends to strike for people (consider the proverbial "mid-life crisis") in the form of divorce, career dissatisfaction, disease, burnout, the resurfacing of unresolved childhood trauma, financial crisis, failing relationships with children, and so forth. One statistic that displays this: the average consumer of self-help products is between the ages of forty and fifty. I'm not saying self-help content is the only or best way for everyone to learn mindfulness and awareness concepts; I'm just highlighting a common pattern in society when it comes to intentional personal growth: the people doing it are often the ones who have already had something traumatic happen to them or who are already facing a problem.

We cannot wait for disaster to strike. These concepts and coping strategies should be introduced earlier in life for increased preventative clarity. Let's say you meet the love of your life at twenty-four and get married. At this time, you know very little about your communication gaps, how your past traumas have affected you, the benefits of therapy and healing, how to keep a relationship healthy, and how to identify red flags before marriage. You bypass this lack of understanding out of ignorance or because you assume your love can just overcome all these issues that are lurking beneath the surface (and I promise they're bound to reach the surface). Your marriage starts great, but after years (or decades) of being with one another, the relationship grows toxic and ends in divorce. You're devastated. Out of desperation to understand what went wrong, you do a deep dive into self-improvement to learn more about yourself and how love, sex, marriage, and relationships operate. Learning and healing at any stage in life is great, and I'm not anti-divorce either. The point is, no one *wants* to get divorced. No one *wants* traumatic and painful experiences, and I think some of these experiences can be avoided.

Had you learned to express your emotions through EQ practices, you might have been able to communicate and access empathy for your partner more effectively and with less anger . . . Had you and your partner put in the work to heal from childhood trauma instead of dragging it into your relationship, the relationship might have deepened authentically . . . Had you known how to be more intentional with your decision-making and understanding around how to create a life you enjoy, you might have avoided feelings of dissatisfaction or resentment . . . Overall, things might have turned out different—less "what ifs," less mayhem, and less pain—or at least your struggles may have happened with increased clarity and peace, had you known and practiced these concepts at an earlier age, before you put on that suit or gown and stuck a ring on your finger.

I don't want young people to wait for something bad to happen that forces them to stitch up their wounds. Instead, get prepared and try to avoid certain wounds altogether. Although adversity is truly inevitable, some of it can be avoided through the power of increased intention. Life will always be uncertain, but improved clarity and mindset, starting now, will make navigating all the adventures to come, no matter how joyous or stressful, so much easier and more satisfying.

## A Short Burst of Science

Science backs up what I'm saying as well. I won't dig crazy deep into this, but let's take a moment to look at the early development of EQ practices from a purely scientific perspective.

Your brain is a complex system of neurological pathways; you can think of it as a complex system of roads. The more you travel down a specific set of roads to get from point A to point B, the more that pathway is ingrained into your mind. You can probably remember the exact route you took to get from your home to your high school. Not just the right and left turns, but the details: what the trees looked like, what the houses looked like, how many traffic lights there were. You probably can't recall that amount of detail for the road route to a concert venue you've only been to twice.

The more we use specific neurological pathways, the more we drive those routes, the more ingrained they become. This is how habits and behavioral patterns are formed: through the strengthening of specific neurological pathways. You've probably heard someone say, "I'm a little rusty," when they haven't done something in a while. We feel "a little rusty" because the neural pathway for that task or skill hasn't been used in a while and is depleted in size and strength. Using it becomes a more conscious process.

As we age, our habits and behavioral patterns become more ingrained into our brains. That's why it's so important we start intentionally choosing the neurological pathways we consistently use, or drive down, now; it will be much more painful and disruptive to rewire our minds thirty years from now, when our mental habits have become much more ingrained and our brains are less elastic. Have you ever tried to change a seventy-five-year-olds mind? It can be almost impossible because they've been strengthening the same neural pathways for years, becoming set in their ways, their habits, and their mindsets.

Let's consider an example. Harriett grew up with very neurotic parents. Anytime there was a conflict between her parents, she'd hear them ranting to friends, or even to her, about it for weeks. Frustration and anger were an overarching theme of her parent's relationship, and they carried that negative energy with them all day every day whether they were physically together or not.

Harriett takes on these behavioral patterns as a child and carries them into her adulthood. As a fifty-two-year-old woman, Harriett has lost more friends than she can count because of the constant gossiping behind their back and the awful, negative energy she consistently radiates. She has stomach issues because she's constantly stressed and upset. She's tried therapy, but she simply can't imagine any other way to function. This behavioral pattern of becoming over-obsessed and focused on minor inconveniences and conflicts is quite literally ruining her life. The constant state of anger is tearing her apart.

Harriett is not at all a bad person; she just doesn't know any better. She is acting in relation to trauma responses and learned behaviors. While that's normal and in no way shameful, if she wants a better life, she'll need to change. Of course, it's very possible for Harriet to make positive changes now as an adult, but imagine if Harriett had been taken aside as a child, teen, or in her twenties. Had she worked on making these healthy changes sooner rather than later, her behavioral habits could have been adjusted much more easily.

## The Sooner You Know

This book is not titled sooner or never. We can change at any stage of life. But twenty-two years of hardwired software is much easier to adjust than fifty-two years of it. That's why the message of this book is so urgent, because, truly, the sooner you know, the better.

In my journey of writing this book, a lot of people, especially older people, did not like the concept of a young adult writing a personal growth book. Again and again, I heard things like: "You're too young," "You have to age to know how to grow," "You only know this stuff because of what you went through as a kid." All incorrect.

Just like any other skill, emotional intelligence, an improved mindset, and mindfulness are skills that can be taught and learned by and to any person of any age. I'm not writing this book because I've experienced traumatic events or because I'm just an "old soul." The development of mental maturity depends much more on intentional learning and practice than it lies on how many years you've been alive. As I mentioned earlier, I've been studying this stuff for years. I love it. It's my passion. I want to relay what I've learned and experienced to an audience that I understand. As teens and twentysomethings, we're going through similar struggles and similar experiences.

That being said, we are constantly evolving. So, feel free to pick and choose the elements from this book that best resonate with you now. You can always come back to it later for more context as you grow and change. My hope is that you'll intentionally incorporate at least a few things from this book into your life to help you change for the better. And that maybe the following twenty-three chapters will help you feel a little less alone in this ridiculous emerging adult journey. This book is not just a collection of practices and knowledge but a vulnerable manifesto of who I was, who I am, and who I am working to become.

To sum up my "why" for writing this book: I wrote this book to make other young adults feel less alone by exposing my humanity. I wrote this book to create a community of incredible young people who want to develop alongside one another. I wrote this book to inspire others to lead and love. I wrote this book to create a support system for young people who don't have one. I wrote this book to help you understand how intrinsically sublime you are. I wrote this book to tell you that we are not the future as we are often told, we are the present *and* the future. I wrote this book to empower you.

## What to Expect

As we start this journey together, you can expect three things out of this book:

### Thing 1
An ability to identify **social constructs** that negatively impact the general population. These conditionings and pressures begin in your youth. You'll learn how their damaging side effects can extend into your adulthood. Once we identify these unhealthy thought patterns, I'll explain how we can unlearn and combat them.

### Thing 2
Exercises, practices, and a developed understanding of ways to improve your state of **being**. Concepts that will allow you to have a healthier relationship with yourself and others.

### Thing 3
Guidance and knowledge on how to improve your experience going forward when it comes to decision-making, goal-setting, and action-taking. How to better navigate the **doing** and designing of your life.

# PART ONE

# Unlearning Unhelpful Social Constructs

There are a lot of ideas and beliefs passed around in our society about what your teen and twentysomething years are supposed to look like. These ideas about how society feels we are supposed to live this portion of our life leave many of us disoriented and fearful.

Welcome to part one, I'll be your tour guide. If you check your map, we've got four stops to unlearning the BS society crammed down your throat. Each stop contains a social construct that we need to unpack so we can make the most out of our travel through life. Unlearning is just as important as learning because you've only got limited space in your suitcase. If you cram that suitcase too full, it gets really heavy to lug around.

Lastly, I want you to know that I'm here as your tour guide because I truly care about how your trip goes and I wholeheartedly believe in your ability to make your life extraordinary.

The first stop: "A Three-Course Meal of BS"

Don't want you to be hungry during our trip, so I'd thought we'd stop at Life's BS Café to start.

# 1

# A Three-Course Meal of BS

**Y**our teens, and especially twenties, come with a lot of age-related pressures. These pressures are something we could definitely do without; there is enough pressure and stress as is. To begin, I want to help in releasing us from these unnecessary weights on our back. Below I've laid out a three-course meal of social constructs that cause immense pressure at this age that we can work towards releasing ourselves from. When it comes to your personal growth process, unlearning what doesn't serve us is just as important as learning what does.

## The BS Appetizer: "The Best Time of Your Life"

Your teens and twenties are extremely glamorized by the media and society. It's, frankly, very harmful. You're told "high school and college are supposed to be the best times of your life." Said who? When did we decide on that? Because I sure as hell know I wasn't a part of that meeting. I can't speak for everyone, but I've found many young people are really sick of people telling them this is supposed to be the best time of their life.

If you are a teen or twentysomething who is battling with mental illness, feelings of loneliness, confusion, sadness, overbearing stress, or excruciating pressure, you're not alone. You are not doing life wrong; you've just hit a natural rough patch. Emphasize *natural*.

If you are in high school, college, a limbo in-between stage, or just trying to get by at the moment and simply aren't having a good time, it's natural. Once again, you are not doing it wrong; you're just dealing with the cards you've been dealt. Don't compare this stage of your life to anyone else's.

Somewhere in Utah, 2012. I was eleven years old. Tall, lanky, middle bangs, red hair, and probably wearing some sort of sweat outfit with pink and white Nike Shox. My Nana had decided to help my older sister and I each plant a small flower garden in our backyard. We both got to pick what flowers went into our individual mini gardens. I instantly picked Snapdragons, along with a few others. They'd been my favorite flower for years, ever since my mom had showed me that they could be turned into mini-opera singers! She'd position the Snapdragon between her thumb and her pointer finger and pinch its sides. As the mouth of the flower opened, my mom would sing out a tune. Coolest thing I'd ever seen. Google "Snapdragon singing," and you'll get a fuller understanding of what I'm talking about here.

A Home Depot trip, some digging, watering, and a sunburn later my garden was complete. I asked my Nana how long it would take for the flowers in my garden to bloom as I was really looking forward to having my own singing, Snapdragons. She told me each one would sprout and bloom at different times, but if I cared for them, they'd all bloom eventually.

At each stage of life, we will all be at different stages of our growing process. It wouldn't make any sense if we potted a bunch of different flowers and expected them all to bloom at once. A Marigold takes about eight weeks to grow and a Pansy takes about one to three weeks to grow. Just because the Pansy was further in its growing process doesn't mean we ask, "What the heck is wrong with the Marigold?" We naturally assume that the Marigold is in a different stage of its life at that moment—a stage of its life that is equally as important. Just because the Marigold doesn't look outwardly as beautiful as the Pansy yet, doesn't mean it isn't beautiful or won't be beautiful. The Marigold is just a different flower. If you're young and feel like your life isn't going as you expected or frankly, just kind of sucks right now: IT'S OKAY. Just because someone else's flower has already started to bloom, doesn't mean yours won't. It just means you're a different flower. Plain and simple. Keep being resilient, watering yourself, surrounding yourself with nutrient-rich experiences and people, and remember that everyone's plant grows differently and not to mention was dropped in different soil.

Let me dish out some tough love for a second. If we wind up on our death beds and pronounce our time as teens and early twentysomethings thee absolute best time of our life, I'd dare to say we didn't live our life very well.

If we only thrived in a time of our life where time is abundant and responsibility, for many, hasn't quite hit its peak, there is probably an issue in how we're living. If we can't learn to make our life beautiful as time and responsibility fluctuate, we've failed to adapt. We've failed to learn how to take control of the reins of the day-to-day. If I'm not on my deathbed relaying each segment of my life and the beauty each area brought, I'll feel a lot of regret. We must learn to embrace our ability to take initiative. Embrace responsibility. Embrace the creation of our life.

Remember that no one else but you gets to decide the best time of your life. Although high school and college-aged years are a great time for growth, for many people, this shit is sucking, or it did suck. So many people aren't having a good time, and they feel like there is something wrong with them. We wonder why so many young people struggle with their mental health and feel isolated and it's because they always feel like they're doing it wrong. I'm here to tell you, you are not doing it wrong.

Let's do away with this "best years of your life" stuff. Truly this is going to be one of the hardest times of our lives to navigate, but the beauty of it is that it is a monumental sweet spot for growth and starting to understand who we are. Every time of your life brings new opportunity, experience, and connections. We don't need to glamorize one portion of it. I choose to believe that there is no "best time of life." Your whole life can be beautiful if you choose to make it that way.

**The BS Main Course: You're Twenty-Five? Game Over Kid.**
Not only is there a societal pressure for this to be the best time of our life, but it also often feels like this is the *only* time of our life.

After twenty-five or thirty, we're told it's game over. You're basically dead at that point. Didn't achieve that? Game over. Didn't get married or have kids? You never will. Didn't travel the entire planet? Have fun staying in your hometown forever, kid.

The crazy thing is that the age for when your life is over seems to be getting younger and younger. I recently watched the movie, "Tick, Tick... BOOM" that came out on Netflix. (Amazing, by the way. Lin-Manuel Miranda and Andrew Garfield killed it.) It's based on an early 2000s musical written by Jonathan Larson. The movie is set in the 90s and is about a young, New York-based composer trying to make it in the entertainment industry. One of the main themes of the movie is about life ending at thirty. Jonathan, the main character, feels that if he doesn't get his big Broadway break by his thirtieth birthday, he will have failed. He'll go from a composer working at a diner to a waiter with a music hobby. He thinks of all the greats he looks up to and how they took off at twenty-two . . . twenty-five . . . twenty-seven . . . and he's panicked about it!

As I watched this movie, I kept thinking to myself, "I wish I had till thirty . . ." Sure, in the 90s, any chance of achieving your dreams seemed like it died at thirty. Now it's twenty-five. The world moves 10x faster now. Twenty-one-year-olds are becoming millionaires or societal-changing activists everywhere I turn.

For a young creator, the pressure feels even worse. I think to myself, "If I don't get this book out and make six figures before my twenty-second birthday, I'll have failed." I know I shouldn't feel that way, but sometimes I do, and you probably do, too. Sure, it doesn't make sense for me to have to accomplish all that three years before I can legally rent a car, but that's how it feels sometimes. Honestly, "twenty-two" just doesn't have the same ring to it as "she accomplished x, y, & z by twenty-one."

Millennials: Thirty was the new thirty-five
Gen Z: Twenty-five is the new thirty
Gen ?: Twenty-one will probably be the new twenty-five

That last one is already underway; twenty-one being the new twenty-five. Since I can already feel it myself, and you probably can, too, the next generation is going to get mauled by it. It's awful.

I want you to take this moment to release yourself of that nauseating age-related pressure. Take a deep breath and allow yourself to release that anxiety and fill your heart with compassion, self-love, and patience.

One of my favorite affirmations: "I am at peace with my past, present, and future."

Your life will unravel at its own pace and is absolutely not over at 25 or 30. No more comparing yourself to everyone else's progress.

Another way to curb this idea of thinking that life ends in your mid to late twenties, is to set a goal now to always stay curious and enthusiastic about what life has to offer.

Another movie I watched recently was called "Julie and Julia." It's a true story about a 21st-century woman, Julie, who decides to complete Julia Child's 1960's, 524-recipe cookbook, "Mastering the Art of French Cooking," in 365 days. The movie simultaneously relays Julia Child's, the cookbook authors, idea to pursue the mastery of cooking at age thirty-six. Julia graduated from the world-famous Cordon Bleu cooking school at thirty-nine and published her first cookbook at forty-nine. This cookbook that she created alongside two other women became a best seller and set Julia on her path to be a well-known award-winning, TV personality, author, and chef.

Ernestine Shepherd is an American bodybuilder. She began her bodybuilding at fifty-six. Since she began, she has won two national bodybuilding contests and run nine marathons.

Now eighty-four, she continues to have discipline over her eating habits, works out daily, runs eighty miles a week, and inspires middle-aged and older women that their life isn't over. That age is simply just a number.

Julia and Ernestine are perfect examples of being ambitious in all areas of our lives. To start new projects in our thirties, forties, fifties, sixties, seventies.

Make a goal for yourself right now that you won't stop getting outside your comfort zone, setting new goals, indulging in new experiences, and learning new skills after thirty-five or forty.

Be curious. You'll get out of life what you put into it. Decide at this moment that you will always stay curious.

**The BS Dessert: You Have to Look Twenty-Five ... Forever.** The cherry on top to all this "create your best memories and achieve everything you can possibly dream of in your twenties" talk is the idea that we also need to *look* like we're in our twenties, forever! This societal glamorization of always looking young and baby smooth seems so unreasonable to me. Plus, I'm already at a disadvantage, y'all. I came out of the womb with eyebags, and I don't have anywhere near the budget of J-Lo.

I think we can all get some good out of unlearning this necessity to age backwards. I don't say this because I feel there is anything wrong with wanting to look younger or doing preventative aging work. What I'm trying to get at is that when we're young, we often want to look older, and when we're older, we want to look younger. In life, we always seem to want what we don't have, and sometimes it brings peace to just find beauty in what we do have. If this societal pressure to age backwards gets burdensome or stressful to you, this is me giving you the nudge to remove that pressure from your shoulders.

In my opinion, wrinkles and aging are beautiful and should be treated as such. They tell a story. We end up looking old for a reason. When our bodies age, I believe that look is associated with and radiates stories, experience, and wisdom. Embrace that. It's so beautiful. When my boobies are dragging on the floor, I'll know they represent the kids that I raised. That love and nurture I shared. The long nights with a crying baby that I somehow loved more than anything else in the world. My feet will be old and curled representing the places I've been, the moments I've witnessed, and the world I've explored. My hands will be frail from a lifetime of hard work, service, play, and will represent all my triumphant accomplishments. An aging body is a sign of a complicated, delightful life lived.

Feel free to scrape all three of these BS age-related pressures off your plate. You've got enough to worry about as is. This doesn't need to be "the best time of your life." It's not game over at twenty-five. And you don't have to age backwards if that's not your preference.

# 2

# "Young and Dumb"

As an author of a self-help book, you can imagine I've read, listened to, and studied a lot of self-improvement content myself. I've checked out the whole spectrum of this content, from the "Raa-Raa!" happy stuff to the cognitive-based and research-backed information.

I did all this for a time to improve and heal myself, but later it became my curiosity and desire to figure out what was missing. How could I improve all the self-help information people were internalizing every day, all over the world? I mentioned a bit of what I found in my preface, one point being that young people, like you and I, weren't being talked to directly enough. Coming to that conclusion, I asked myself "Why? Why not teens and twentysomethings?"

The answer to "Why not us?" had a lot of contributing factors, but the factor that bothered me the most was the idea that we just weren't ready for this information. That we as teens and twentysomethings are just too young and immature to get it. No one says that directly, of course, because it's all a subconscious thought process, and this does not relate to all leaders in this space by any means. That being said, the lack of information catered to us in this space has nothing to do with us; it has to do with a societal stereotype.

Generally, the leaders teaching mindset, mindfulness, and EQ are in their forties to sixties. If a forty-five-year-old considered themselves really dumb and unintentional as a college student or young adult, why would they write a book trying to speak to that kid? That kid probably wouldn't listen, right? It makes total sense. But what if that kid was ready to listen, but no one took the time to talk to them? I can't tell you how many times I've heard or read sentiments within this space that were something along the lines of "I'm glad my mindset isn't the way it was in college or I'd be miserable"; "I was so dumb in high school, haha"; or "the only thing I could think about at twenty-five was getting to Friday, hooking up, and finding the next party to go to."

Because you're young, you're an idiot, and that's the way you're supposed to be. That's the way you inherently are. This is what social conditioning has taught many generations to buy into. Society has conditioned generation after generation of young adults to believe that they are less capable of mindful intention, personal growth, or a developed maturity at this point in their lives because they are not fully developed, or they haven't experienced enough yet. What's extremely incorrect about this narrative is an improved mindset, emotional intelligence, and an ability to be mindful doesn't require life experience. It doesn't even require struggle or trauma. These things can be taught and studied. What if we weren't just "young & dumb" or mentally miserable during this early time period of life? What if we developed who we are as the seeds of our lives were being planted? What if we stopped letting ourselves off the hook just because of our age?

Some of you might be thinking: *well, isn't being young and dumb at this age scientifically proven*? I'm sure some of you have heard the statistic that the human brain doesn't fully develop until around your mid-twenties. During early adulthood, you see the final development of the prefrontal cortex. This area of your brain is associated with planning, problem-solving, and other related tasks. But this is precisely why we need to intentionally develop our brains now while the neurological pathways are still extremely malleable, as I mentioned in the introduction.

There is a better way to train our brains while they develop so we don't have to untrain them as much later in life. This training, I believe, starts with exploring who we are and how we interact with the world and how to improve those aspects of ourselves; understanding how to communicate better, understanding your personality and subconscious thought processes, dealing with limiting beliefs, and starting to take steps that will heighten your social and personal awareness.

Sure, recklessness can be fun, especially at this age. Less responsibility, fewer consequences. I get it. It can't be the only thing we manifest right now, though; it often results in loneliness, confusion, and feelings of wasted potential. Do we have to be only crazy and immature in our youth? If you don't want to be, the answer is no. Why does it matter, though, if you choose recklessness with zero second thoughts about intention? Because this is precisely the time of our lives when we have to make a lot of our most crucial decisions on top of the finalization of our brain development.

We can't simply accept this societal idea that emerging adults are often immature idiots, and they couldn't possibly start a healing or growth process yet. Our teens and twenties, despite common beliefs, are not a time to only be careless. It's a crucial time for being intentional. We need to stop letting ourselves off the hook. The answers we seek about our future won't fall into our lap. We need to put in the work. We are more than "young and dumb."

Still not feeling quite urgent for you? Here are some statistics that might be a much-needed wake-up call:

- Eighty-five percent of life's most defining moments take place by age thirty-five.
- Lifetime wage growth increases the most by age thirty.
- We're most likely to meet our partner by age twenty-six, and more than 50 percent of people find the person they will marry in their twenties.
- Our personality changes the most in our twenties; more so than at any other time in our life.

These statistics are not an end all, and correlation does not equal causation. I do not want to enforce the idea that life ends at thirty or thirty-five with these statistics. I'm just trying to make the point that a lot of important stuff often (but definitely not always) goes on in the next five, ten, or fifteen years, and how we navigate it starts with the state of mind we are in. The sooner we can expand mentally and emotionally, the better.

I believe the teens and twentysomethings of this day are ready to listen and hear this personal growth information. In my opinion, today's young people are some of the most amazing, emotionally mature, open-minded generations we've seen yet. We are the perfect generation to break the cycle of unhealed parenting, explosive behavior, interacting with a lack of empathy, cutting down the statistic of marriage only having a 50/50 chance of actually working out, living unfulfilling lives, etc. We can break the generational cycle of low emotional intelligence and a lack of a healthy mindset. If we can learn how to be more growth-oriented now, we can carry this into our relationships and parenting styles. We could literally change the way society functions for generations to come.

You are not just young and dumb, and I won't let you off the hook when it comes to personal growth and self-reflection. I don't want you to let yourself off the hook either because, although it's hard, consciously improving who you are will improve your current and future life in a million different ways. You're ready for more purposeful growth. The fact that you're reading this book shows you probably already know that.

# 3

# "You Are the Future"

A message to my fellow young dreamers or ambitious folk:

I've been hosting my podcast, "Today is the Future," for more than two years now. On my podcast, I interview teens and twentysomethings from all over the world who have an inspiring story to tell. Musicians, artists, filmmakers, entrepreneurs, creatives, activists share with me what goes on behind the scenes in pursuing and achieving things that light their souls on fire. I find my podcast to be such a perfect place for young adults to break through the "perfection" of social media and learn from one another's stories.

If I've learned one thing from interviewing these individuals, it's that age really is just a number. Age does not directly correlate to experience, talent, skill, passion, or success.

Many young people are told they're the future, they're the up-and-coming, but I'd like to change that to we are the present *and* the future.

Today is the future.

The world can be changed by young minds, and the world needs young minds to change it.

You don't have to wait for the future to take action towards your dreams or to create change if you don't want to. If your age is holding you back from pursuing something that you are passionate about, that's not a very strong reason. If anything, it's probably a front for the real reason you haven't pursued that project or idea: you're scared. I get it. I'm scared all the time, but what I've learned on my own journey and from my podcast guests is that if you're scared now, you'll probably be scared in the future, too. You'll be just as scared at thirty as you are at twenty. If anything, you'll be more scared. Waiting is not serving you.

Feeling too young for your opinion to be heard? Speak out anyway.

Feeling unqualified to apply for a specific job or opportunity? Apply for it anyway.

Feeling like the answer will definitely be no? Ask anyway.

All these are feelings, not necessarily reality. This short, motivational blurb is to remind those of you who need to hear it to think big and aim high, and that if there is a perfect time to do that, it's now. If there is an exceptional time to experiment, dream big, or even fail, it's now. This is me rooting for you now.

# 4

# If I Can Just ... Then I'll be Happy

This morning I headed to a coffee shop to rewrite this chapter for the third or fourth time. There were a few chapters in this book that really gave me a run for my money and for one reason or another—this was one of them.

After I ordered, I scanned the room for a place to sit. Packed. This shop is by multiple colleges, and it's finals week right now, so I'm not sure why I was surprised. A statistics major and a retired teacher from Minnesota were kind enough to let me have a seat at their table. I struck up a conversation with the woman next to me, the retired teacher from Minnesota. If you know me, you know I love a good conversation with a stranger. As she and I started to chat, I had such a strong urge to end the conversation and continue with my writing. Not because I wanted to, but because I felt like I needed to. If I wasn't working; I was wasting my time.

At that moment, I thought to myself, "Ya know what Livi, getting this chapter written thirty minutes sooner won't fill your cup today more than allowing yourself to have a fun, thirty--minute coffee shop conversation." We talked for a while, shared book recommendations, and stories, and then she headed out. I hopped back on my computer feeling energized by the interaction and got started working.

Why share this simple interaction with you? As I've started this journey of working for myself and structuring my own time, I've learned that if I don't allow myself the simple moments to interact with a stranger at a coffee shop, or meditate for fifteen minutes, or hang out with friends on a Friday night, or watch a movie I've been wanting to see, all the goals I'm chasing become pointless. Our happiness relies on simple things—not whether we've published a book, got our degree, made a lot of money, or won an award. Sure, reaching our monetary goals can provide convenience and more comfortable living. Reaching our professional or passion-driven goals can bring fulfillment or excitement, too, but long-lasting happiness lies in the little moments, not the big ones. You know the quote; I know the quote. "It's not the journey; it's the destination." So cliché, ugh, I know, but it speaks nothing but the truth. If you want a warm, happy, lightweight feeling when you go to bed at night, grant yourself permission to be present in the simple moments.

As a highly motivated, ambitious person I've had periods of time where I refused to allow myself to talk to that stranger in the coffee shop, even though that's what I wanted to do because it brings me joy. Not gifting myself those simple moments to fuel my soul, didn't help me. It hurt me.

If I've learned one thing from all the self-help books, personal growth podcasts, and interviews with people who have reached incredible professional success, it's that you will not be happier once you achieve x, y, & z. Sure you and I might agree with this on a surface level, but it's pretty hard to believe that achieving more won't make us happier people. It's true. You might become happier as you achieve your goals because you become more in tune with yourself, learned more self-control, or have new high-energy people entering your life, but achievements in and of themselves will not add to your joy in the long-term. If we don't learn how to find joy and be present on the voyage to achieving or attaining x, y, & z, we'll probably turn out to be unhappy people with just a bit more money or medals.

It's so much easier said than done, though. It's easy to look at social media and think, "damn, if I just had that or looked like that, then I'd be happy." Society moves extremely fast around us, and it's very easy to get caught up in it all. Self-love and not feeling like we need x, y, & z to be happy has truly become a rebellious act, especially in today's western culture. I struggle with not getting my worth or happiness wrapped up in my achievements or money. I have to *constantly* check my ego and my values. It's hard.

Now the question is if we don't set our focus on achieving or attaining, where do we set it? Where can we focus ourselves each day to have long-lasting happiness in this life? Yes, being present and giving yourself moments of true joy is a piece of that, but the answer to feeling full of light and love lies in our ability to live in alignment.

You'll see me mention living in alignment a lot in this book, but what does that mean? Living in alignment means that we've aligned our actions, priorities, and energy output with our core values. We've let our conscious self and the desires of our soul or heart lead us, as opposed to our subconscious mind and the desires of our ego.

## What Does Living in Alignment Feel Like?

It feels calm and peaceful. It feels warm and kind. Aligning our actions and thoughts with our values and our truest selves feels like freedom. The freedom to grant ourselves permission to show up as who we truly are. When you're living in alignment, there is an enduring aura of balance despite the highs and lows of life.

Now you know what living in alignment looks like and feels like, why would you want that? Sure, this chapter is about happiness and joy, but I think what we all actually want is peace. The things we desire won't bring peace. Our desires are unquenchable, you desire one thing, you get it, and you'll probably desire another thing. Being at peace is the result of staying in alignment.

## How Do We Live In Alignment?

Above I said, "Being at peace is the result of living in alignment." The keyword here is "being." We improve our state of being. We assess or reassess what our values and priorities are.

We act in accordance with those things and live from a place of worthiness and love. Our ability to do that comes through healing, learning, unlearning, mindfulness, and becoming truly present. To give all this living in alignment stuff more clarity, let me put it into the context of my own life.

My dad was a very money-driven man. He had an incredibly lovely soul, but he battled his unquenchable desires his entire life. His internal struggles were very apparent in the energy that radiated from him. As his daughter, I inherited a lot of that energy. In true transparency, I have a deeply rooted, insatiable desire for money and achievement, as a lot of us do. But for years I watched those same desires tear him apart, absolutely destroying his ability to have peace. I decided I wanted to unlearn this mental idea of being driven by such finite desires. So, I asked myself where I could redirect my focus. If I can't measure the success of my life or my actions based on my net worth or achievements, how else will I do it? I turned to the opposite of desire: peace. How much peace I felt in a given moment would become my measuring stick. Not lack of sadness, anxiety, or stress, as we'll always feel those things at times, but peace. The question was how could I make peace be the underlying essence of it all. I knew peace was the goal because when I'm at peace I have ten times the capacity to experience joy, to appreciate life, and to be present. How do I keep peace in my heart, mind, and soul? By living in alignment. That's my goal now, and that's how I gauge my success: how well I'm living in alignment.

Now, when I get caught up in reaching my goals, I habitually lean back on that question. Are you in alignment, Livi? Okay, then you're killing it. Making my life goal to live in alignment allows me to keep my desires at bay because I truly have nothing more I need to attain. If I died next week, I'd be at peace. I'd know I was living as aligned and as true to who I am as I possibly could, and that's a beautiful feeling. The goal has been reached. I'm no longer reaching or longing. I've found myself. I've found Livi, and I live aligned with the purest, most peaceful, and joyful version of her. It's freakin' dope. Learning to be at peace through alignment is dope.

My warning to you here is to unlearn the idea of needing to have, attain, or achieve x, y, or z to be happy. I'm telling you now that I know and you know that x, y, and z aren't what will bring you joy and peace, despite how much society layers on the idea that it will.

Our goal is to live aligned. If we can do that, we've won.

In the next two chapters, we'll cover two tactics we can use to unpack these social constructs and make the most of our teens and twenties: self-control and mindfulness.

# 5

# Flying Takes More
# Than Pixie Dust

A lack of self-control doesn't make you free; it prevents you from attaining true freedom. Immediate gratification is different from freedom.

What is self-control and why do we need it?

Growing up I remember one lesson my mom loved to teach us. She called it the funnel analogy. She somehow managed to give a lot of my friends the funnel analogy talks, too. You just can't stop Mama Leah from spreading the love.

The analogy goes as follows: She would explain that a lot of times kids and teenagers think they're being limited by their parents' rules or things they're told they probably shouldn't do. I'm talking about the house rules that are reasonable and meant to keep you safe. Don't do hard drugs, don't drive without a seatbelt, don't let your grades drop, don't stay out too late, don't run with scissors, and so on and so forth. When given these rules, we often found ourselves thinking they were just limiting us, giving us less choices, and stifling our fun. You probably thought at some point growing up that you'd do better without the rules or the long talks giving you advice about why you shouldn't put firecrackers in your brother's bed.

Here's what my mom told me about following these rules: let's maybe not call them rules, but making better, more reasonable decisions. If you make better choices while you're young, it gives you more choices as you get older. We need to make decisions not just with the current version of ourselves in mind, but also the future version of ourselves in mind. She told me if I controlled myself now, I wouldn't have to clean up so many pieces later. I wouldn't end up ruining family relationships, having a child in high school, ending up in rehab, going to jail, etc. If you make too many wild, irrational decisions that can create unwanted outcomes like the ones I've listed, your options will be lessened. The paintbrush that you shape your life with gets stiffer because you're trying to recover from choices you made when you were young. So, if you give yourself some restrictions now (make your funnel a little smaller), your funnel will be opened up as the years roll by. As much as I'd like to think I'm indestructible, I'm not.

## Self-Control Is Freedom

You're standing on the edge of a bridge. You look down and see the water and are working up the courage to jump. You have on a harness, and a bungee cord is wrapped around your ankles. You signed up for this, and you are dang sure going to be getting your money's worth, no turning back. You're nervous as you inch closer to the edge and stare at the long drop below, but excitement and adrenaline follow your anxiety that is battling to take the reins.

And then you jump.

You're falling. The wind is running past your face, and you are so proud of yourself for working up the courage. You feel like you're really living, like you're flying. Just before the water, the bungee catches you. You shoot back up screaming, but also having the experience of a lifetime. Your momentum slows, and you're ready for round two.

So, what allowed the experience to be so extraordinary when it was over and you look back at it? What kept you from hitting the water? The bungee cord. The bungee cord allowed you to fly. The bungee cord represents the self-control you implement into your life. When you restrict yourself from things that don't benefit you, things that slow your progression, you are putting the bungee cord on. You are allowing yourself to fall and enjoy the feeling of flying, instead of panicking while you fall. Red Bull isn't the only thing that gives you wings my friend.

But are there times where you think you're putting on the bungee cord, but are really stepping backwards from the edge of the bridge, driving home, and so to speak "not getting your money's worth?" Is there something you wish you could do, but something always stops you from pursuing it, from flying? Now look at that thing a little deeper. Is something stopping you, or are you stopping yourself?

We tell ourselves hundreds of lies throughout our lives, and often these lies can become our truth. Before I wrote this book, I had identified my lies. I was telling myself that I was too young, unqualified, inexperienced, and that I didn't have the capacity to make it happen. I told myself these lies because if I never tried, I figured I'd never fail. If I didn't manifest my goal to write a book, no one would question my abilities. I thought these lies were keeping me safe. I thought they were my bungee cord. They weren't. They were letting me fall right to the water of regret. Later on in this book I'll give you some more insight on how to identify, understand, and address the lies that are boxing you in. Caging you like an eagle in a chicken coop. You have tremendous power and potential, but you have to stop trying to reel it in. Let it fly. I want nothing more than to see you fly.

If you aren't too young to make an impact, then you aren't too young to take control. Self-control will allow you to make an impact and shape your life into what you want it to be.

# 6

# The Perfect Bag
# of Popcorn

For the year I was in college, I lived in the dorms. Let me tell you, dorms . . . not the move. Did not like those. Why are dorms not the move? The food, and sure there were other factors I wasn't quite a fan of, but the food was definitely up there on my list. The food was not good. A person can only eat so many Chinese chicken salads and orders of beef broccoli from Panda Express.

I'm a big believer in eating healthy and fueling your body correctly. In high school, I had no idea how badly I was actually eating before I started researching it. When I had lived at home, prior to college, I cooked a lot and meal-prepped on Sundays. I would plan what I was going to eat the following week, go to the store on Saturday and get what I needed, and cook it all on Sunday. But when I got to the dorms, eating healthy was not easy, especially when I had bags of peanut M&M's staring me in the face every time I checked out. I was on a required meal plan, and not a cheap meal plan, I might add, so I had to eat what was available. I rarely got a good serving of steamed broccoli, asparagus, or green beans, and if I did, it was most likely drenched in butter, sauce, or oil. Never in my life had I had vegetable withdrawals. It just wasn't like what I cooked for myself at home. I missed cooking so much that I'd go to the store and get sad walking down the olive oil aisle.

One thing I started eating a lot of was popcorn. My dorm roommate could have attested to this, along with everyone who lived around me. I started eating popcorn probably five times a week. I ate it quite a bit before college, but it reached a whole other level in the dorms. I was buying the Signature Kirkland popcorn bags in bulk. Eventually I decided I should probably make a switch, so I didn't clog my arteries with salt and butter: I started buying the healthier one-hundred-calorie, snack-size popcorn. It wasn't the worst thing I could have eaten every night, but it wasn't the best, either. Pretty much every weekday, I made the public area by the elevators of our floor smell like popcorn because that's where the microwaves were. People I knew would walk off the elevator onto our floor and know that Livi was, in fact, making popcorn again. When I came home from college, my mom and I decided I should stop with the popcorn addiction. We physically took all the popcorn out of the pantry, put it in a bin, and it still remains hidden somewhere in her house. I stopped cold turkey for a while, joined a support group, and went two months popcorn-free. All right, maybe not the support group part, but I did improve my relationship with popcorn. Now I only eat it occasionally in healthy doses, but I won't lie, as I went through the editing process of this book, my popcorn addiction has started to creep back up on me a bit.

The point is, I will always love popcorn. The thing about popcorn is that there is an art to popping the perfect bag. There is nothing worse than being so excited to eat a bag of popcorn and having it come out burnt, smelling like a Las Vegas casino.

Two rules to the perfect bag of popcorn:

1. Don't get distracted.
2. Listen carefully.

You are a bag of popcorn. Yes, I'm about to get into a corny analogy. (See what I did there? Cornyyy. I'm sorry, I swear, no more dad jokes.) Whether you want to or not, in your late teens and throughout your twenties, you'll have to decide on schooling options, career options, possibly marriage, where to live, people to associate with, and how to manage your time. You'll start receiving a lot of new responsibility. This is why you should care about developing your mindfulness. Mindfulness will allow you to make much more intentional decisions. Before I dive deeper into how the two rules of popcorn popping relates to you, I want to clarify the difference between mindfulness and self-awareness. Being self-aware is a bit simpler. It's not too hard to be aware of where we struggle as people, when we feel "off," or what things we do that probably aren't very good for us mentally. Mindfulness on the other hand requires us to dig deeper, to go beyond the obvious. Mindfulness requires a deeper understanding of who we are on a core level in relation to our values, our passions, what fuels us, and what makes us feel like our best self. Mindfulness requires that we let go of the past, become fully present, and be in touch with our emotions. Mindfulness is about being fully present in our mind, in the present moment. It's not just being aware that you might be unhappy or out of alignment; it's looking inward in this moment and reflecting on the causes of that unhappiness, the roots of your pain, choosing change and growth, and releasing the pain that keeps you living in the past. Mindfulness is healing and taking action. It's becoming comfortable with yourself and loving your ability to be fully present with yourself. Mindfulness requires us to look inside on a soulful, energetic level and choose to listen and realign.

Rule #1: Don't get distracted. Your life is the popcorn in the microwave. If you just let the timer go, leave the microwave on, and hope the popcorn will just turn out the way you want, it's probably going to burn. When you get distracted, or live on auto pilot, and let your life just tick by and don't learn to really be present, you will probably end up in your forties or fifties with a burnt bag of popcorn. You'll take a look at your life—essentially look into the bag of popcorn—and not be very satisfied with the result. Then you have to pick the popcorn apart, find the burnt pieces—maybe your marriage, your career, your eating habits—and fix the life you neglected. We must become present and understanding of what actions will be in our own best interest in this moment. Presence allows for a well-popped bag of popcorn.

Rule #2: Listen carefully, aka mindfulness. As you become a more present person, you must then learn to be aware of your thoughts, your values, and what an aligned life looks like for you. Mindfulness is the art of becoming a more conscious and self-aware person. An empowered person.

You have to be attentive and take the popcorn out as soon as there are three seconds of silence between pops. Before your life starts passing you by, you can train yourself to listen to the pops. You can train your mind to have more clarity and make better decisions. You can learn to be more in tune with who you are and where you really want to end up through self-awareness.

You are more than capable of making a great batch of popcorn, a great life for the present and future you. It's going to take some work though, and some really intense self-reflection. The "how-to" for increasing mindfulness will come in part two of this book. I just want to continue focusing on why mindfulness matters so much at this point in our lives.

If we don't start training our minds now to be more mindful, it's going to be a lot harder to do so later. It's like getting a new puppy. When you get a puppy, you start training him or her as soon as they can walk. You teach puppies to not pee on the carpet, to ask when they need to go outside, to sit, to shake, and that it's bad to eat used tissues out of the garbage. If you neglect training and developing the puppy until he is fully grown, it will be a much harder task to retrain their brain to know that they shouldn't be doing things the way they've been doing them.

That is why you should care now about developing your relationship with yourself and ability to stay mindful. If we don't learn how to be more in tune and present with ourselves now, it will become even harder to train our minds to adjust to this concept later. There will also be a lot of pee-stained carpet to rip out and replace later in our life due to unconsciously made, unaligned decisions.

But no one is going to hold you responsible; only you can decide to start learning how to be in a better mental state—for example, understanding your trauma and the lies that have become your truth, or recognizing the fact that maybe you are kind of a know-it-all or a hothead and that it's something you need to work on, or realizing that you don't know how to set boundaries with the people in your life and usually find yourself getting walked on. These are all areas of mindfulness. Mindfulness allows us to unlock what areas of ourselves require unlearning, relearning, growth, and healing.

Everyone can start understanding themselves better right now, regardless of age. It's time to start stumbling intentionally and stop stumbling mindlessly.

So, to recap part one: understand that you've been socially conditioned or pressured to believe certain ideas that might restrict your potential, and that through mindfulness and self-control we can unlearn those concepts and start to truly understand who we are and what we want out of our lives. We can't live our best lives if we don't learn to work in harmony with our minds first.

# PART TWO

# Being

**P**art one established the concept of unhelpful social constructs that require unlearning through mindfulness and self-control so that our life is authentically designed. To begin this journey of intentionally creating our lives, we must first be in a better state of *being*, mentally and emotionally, before we really get to the *doing* and designing. Part two will teach you practices that will allow you to become a more mindful, empowered, and healthy individual.

# 7

# Becoming Autodidacts

L et me give you a list of three names, and I'd like you to think to yourself what each of these people have in common:

- Frida Kahlo: incredible painter and the creator of conversation for political and feminist movements
- William Shakespeare: one of the greatest English poets to ever exist and who introduced hundreds of new words into the English language
- Henry Ford: a man who helped shape the automobile and manufacturing industries and a world-famous business leader

These three people came from different places and backgrounds, and they gained success in different spaces, but one thing they have in common: autodidacticism. Big word for a simple concept. They were people who were actively self-educated. In other words, an autodidact (auto-die-dact – I had to Google how to say it right myself) is a self-learner. Besides the people I've listed, many other greats who have changed the course of history were often mainly self-educated.

I believe self-education is just as, or even more important, than formal education. To preface, this chapter isn't about being a college hater, because I'm not.

I can't tell you how many times I've been told: "What you do and learn outside of school is what will be most important when getting a job in the future," or "You will learn more during your first year in a fast-paced career setting than you probably will in your four years of college." This is because putting yourself in real-world educational experiences (something that requires you to learn on the go) is one the purest forms of learning. Real-world experiences force you to adapt and push your limits. It's where knowing how to self-educate comes in, but self-educating is also really hard.

Self-education takes motivation, consistency, and diligence, but it also allows for unrestrained creativity, gratification, and clarity. Formal education teaches you *how* to learn. Self-education only works when you've learned how to *love* to learn, which takes more intention because you have no due dates or deadlines. You must be driven by self-discipline and dedication, which is hard and scary at times. Despite that, I think you and I both have the balls to be driven by self-discipline and dedication.

There are two forms of self-education: learning about life and learning about yourself. Both are equally important.

Learning about life involves teaching ourselves skills through articles, websites, books, YouTube videos, trial and error, etc. Some personal examples: learning how to cook vegetable chicken stir-fry instead of eating frozen burritos three meals a day; looking up YouTube videos on how to market a business on Instagram; Googling articles on how to format a job application; or learning out how to rewire your blinkers because you figured it was a good idea to buy a '65 Ford pickup that drinks your gas money (that car was a lot of fun, though, I won't lie). Some of my own self-education came out of necessity, but it's also important to seek self-education when it's not a necessity. That's when you start your personal growth in an exponential rather than linear incline.

Learning about yourself is also just as important. We must take the time to study our actions, mindsets, opinions, and habits. It's important to be self-aware of our emotions, our trauma, our flaws, our truth, and so forth. If we don't do this throughout our lives, it will leave a trail of gunk behind us and will gum up our ability to be truly happy and present. We will talk more about self-awareness and important mindset shifts you can make later on in this book.

It's easy to understand that self-learning drastically improves your personal growth and self-awareness; actually getting yourself to do it is the tricky part. Whatever it is that you've always dreamed of achieving or learning, you can acquire the self-discipline and knowledge to do so. You are worthy of your dream life and can steer your life toward your dreams, starting now. Your success will come through learning to love to learn.

## Success Comes to Those Who Intentionally Seek Out Self-Education

One of the best things about self-driven learning is it can be done with no price tag attached. We live in the era of self-education. Unfortunately, I think that when resources come in abundance, we tend to take advantage of them less often. We can find online classes, YouTube videos, books, podcasts right at our fingertips. We can gain knowledge at an exponential rate through technology. Not only this, millions of people in this world don't have the same access to resources like you might. If you take advantage of the resources you've been given, the universe will open its doors to even more resources and opportunities.

Like I said, those who thirst to learn *will*. And willing students will attract teachers.

Listening to podcasts whenever I work out is one self-education tactic I've loved doing. Try this if you can. A youth leader in my community first told me that she liked to listen to church talks or podcasts while she worked out, and it made absolutely no sense to me. At the time, my mind thought that the rap music I listened to while I worked out would give me the energy I needed, while church talks would not equal workout energy. One day in my junior year of high school, I went to the gym and gave her advice a shot. Instead of shuffling my rap playlist as usual, I went on Spotify and played a self-help podcast, assuming this would be the longest workout experience of my life. Instead, it was probably the shortest. I was listening to Jonathan Fields's "Good Life Project" podcast (go listen to it when you get the chance), one of the first that started my introduction to so many other inspiring, educational, and motivational podcasts I have grown to love over the years. The fact that I was listening to motivational stories and activating my mind gave me the energy to get through the sweat and burning muscles. Now, I can't remember the last time I listened to music at the gym. This simple habit of listening to podcasts while I work out has helped guide my personal development and self-educating journey immensely.

Sounds simple and kind of silly, but it's true.

Start looking for ways you can increase the time you spend self-educating. The time is always there; you just have to give it to yourself. As nerdy as it sounds, I actually get excited to do daily planning now. Once you learn to make time for personal growth that pulls you in the direction of the things you want to achieve, your dreams will come to you much sooner.

You now might be thinking, "Great Livi, so I need to read books, develop tactical skills on my own time, or maybe listen to podcasts on my way to work in the morning, but how do I actually decide on what I want to educate myself on?"

A great place to start is choosing to learn more about things that you already like or interest you. Go get a paper or open a note-taking app on your phone and make a list of at least five things that make you happy or spark your interest. Get specific. Once you identify these little things, pick one and learn a bit more about it.

If the stars make you happy, read a book about the stories behind the constellations. If you love classic cars (aka me), take a shop class or go on YouTube or ask your neighbor who works on cars all day some questions and learn more about how they work. If your grandma's homemade caramels make you happy, go to her house and learn how to make them. If you love watching comedy sets, go watch some interviews about what it actually takes to be an amazing comedian. You'll gain new knowledge and skills and you'll be starting to learn how to love learning.

Consistently self-educating will guide you in the present and help you achieve your dreams in the future.

# 8

# No More ANT-ics

Oh, TikTok. The place where I learn everything I didn't know I needed to know. Because of TikTok, I know the first use of the abbreviation OMG was in 1917. I also know how to cook homemade Butterfingers, which I know I will never do. Among the list of random hacks, fact or cap videos, and the slow disintegration of my sense of humor, TikTok also taught me this:

If you place an ant on a piece of paper and draw a circle around it with a black permanent marker the ant will stay inside the circle. It will no longer go outside the circle you drew around it. I've put this useless information to the test, and it's true. If you don't push the ant outside the circle with your finger, it will stay inside the circle trapped. Of course, I'm not evil, and I showed the ant it could escape, but if I hadn't, it probably would have died in that circle.

Many people spend their entire lives inside of self-drawn, confining circles, deciding there is no escape. We do so because we *think* we can't leave them, when we 100 percent can, just like the ant. We set limitations on ourselves like, "I'm just not smart," or, "I'm always late to everything," or "I always screw stuff up."

These are called limiting beliefs. Belief is defined as "an acceptance that a statement is true or that something exists." The more someone believes that they "always screw stuff up," the more they'll manifest that behavior. The more someone believes that "they aren't a good enough artist," the more opportunity they'll pass up. *Beliefs*, that's all they are – not truths.

These limiting beliefs only become true when we draw that imaginary, entrapping circle around us and decide they're true. Limiting beliefs destroy millions of people's potential every day; don't let yourself be one of those people. No more constraining and confining yourself. You have the power to stop accepting the things in your life or about yourself that aren't serving you. You are the creator of your reality. Let's learn together how to stop self-sabotage and step outside the limiting belief circles we've drawn around ourselves, limiting our ability to flourish.

How do we step outside these limiting belief circles? Simple. Choose a new narrative that you tell yourself. In fact, you can step outside that circle at any moment if you just gain some perspective.

Lizzo, Miss Billboard Charts herself, is amazing at choosing what perspectives she decides to believe. That woman is incredible at choosing narratives that positively serve her and her career.

For example, she was talking on her Instagram story the other day about a comment someone left under her video on TikTok. Basically, in one specific video, she was getting a higher-than-usual amount of comments hating on her weight.

One comment, in particular, said, "Damn, she is so big, imma start calling it 'rolling a Lizzo.' "

When Lizzo first started talking about this comment, my initial reaction was, "Why do people always have to mention her weight, just lay off, geez." Right after I thought that, Lizzo said in her story, "I LOVE THIS. How iconic. 'Rolling a Lizzo,' like rolling a fattie, a fat blunt. That is *everything*. We will only be referring to it as 'rolling a Lizzo' from now on."

After she said that I thought to myself, she's so right hah! "Rolling a Lizzo" could be her version of yelling "Kobe!" when you throw something in the trash. That *is* iconic. I loved this example because she chose to take something that easily could have been seen as negative and created a more positive narrative and belief around it. We are the creators of our story; of the narrative we see.

It is true that society and the biological functions of our mind can put limitations on us, mental illness, physical limitations, systemic racism, sexism, deeply ingrained trauma, etc. There are systems and levels of relatively uncontrollable limitation from our end. For this chapter, I want to focus on what we *can* control. I want to focus on where we *can* find self-empowerment. We put a lot, and I mean A LOT, of limitations on ourselves. Sometimes we don't even recognize we're doing it. Sometimes all we need is perspective.

Not only can we change the narrative we tell ourselves about the world around us like Lizzo, but we can also shift our perspective of what we're truly capable of ourselves.

In 1954, British Olympic athlete, Roger Bannister, was the first person to break the four-minute mile. Roger talked about how in order to achieve this, he had to decide that it was possible. He visualized himself every day crossing the finish line before the clock hit 4:00:00. He accepted and believed the idea that it was possible, and he did it! He was the first Olympian to break the four-minute mile. After he did the impossible, within the next year other athletes started breaking the four-minute mile. All it took was for one athlete to say, "Hey, this impossible four-minute mile thing is something I don't accept. I'm going to walk outside of this limiting belief circle," and then a bunch of athletes followed in his footsteps. He changed his perspective and in turn, changed a lot of other people's perspectives as well.

The first step to breaking our limiting beliefs: we need to decide that we are powerful creators. Having limiting beliefs is like staring at a blank canvas and saying to ourselves, "hmmm I wish that canvas had more color on it," all while having a paintbrush and buckets of paint sitting at the base of the easel. It makes no sense from an outsider's perspective. The paint is right frickin' there – just use it! Our limiting beliefs create a fog that convinces us that there's no paint or no paintbrush in our hand to create our reality.

You may be thinking, I don't really care if the canvas is blank. I don't really care if I always tell myself "I can't," do certain things because it's more comfortable. I like it because it doesn't require change. If you feel this way, I've been where you are at, and let me tell you why it matters that we let these limiting beliefs go.

We *love* a good label, especially in western culture, and we cling to them way too strongly. An outdated personal label is also a form of a limiting belief. Attaching to labels too strongly can destroy us internally. You might label yourself as the 4.0, gifted kid and enter college only to get wrecked by organic chemistry. Your standard 4.0 GPA that semester drops to a 3.5 and you have a complete and utter identity crisis. Unhealthy alert!

We need to allow ourselves the fluidity and grace to change the way we view ourselves, to allow for failure and evolution. To move from "I'm a perfect student," to "I'm someone who tries their best in their studies."

For a very, very long time I told myself I wasn't a very loving person. I decided I wasn't a nurturer, and I wasn't a warm person for others to be around. I decided that I was a colder, logical, and analytical person, and that's just who I was. When I decided I wasn't a loving, warm person, I found myself very unhappy. I had all this beaming love inside with nowhere to put it. Looking back, this choice was a way for me to protect myself from a purer, more vulnerable expression of who I was. It was also a way to make some sense of the juxtaposition of my personality.

The juxtaposition of my personality has been a struggle for me my entire life. Many of you might relate. If you ask anyone really close to me what two colors describe me, surprisingly all of them, ALL of them, say yellow and red. These two colors give off *very* different vibes. With red, you think of, intense, confident, aggression, diligence, dominance; and with yellow, we usually think of happiness, warmth, caution, energy, optimism, intellect. To me, the two seemed fairly contrasting colors to give off.

For so long I felt like I had to be either red or yellow. I found that the more I amplified my yellow, the more warmth I felt but the less serious others took me, and the more I amplified my red, the more I achieved but the less connection I felt with people, which I need as an extrovert. It might seem so simple, but once I really, truly accepted the idea that I could be both, life got way better. I allowed myself to be giddy over cute dog videos, give big hugs, wear colorful sundresses, and sing Disney princess music while I work around the house AND ask for what I want, take up space, default to logic over emotion, wear basketball shorts, and have the capacity for very direct and serious conversations. I could be both. Once I stepped out of the idea that I had to be one or the other, I found my capacity to express love and warmth became much higher. I now let myself cry when my body wants to. I've accepted the fact that I actually do like hugs. I smile as I drive alone in my car. and I talk to strangers in coffee shops or on elevators.

When we remove a rigid idea of who we feel we have to be – these limiting beliefs –we begin to live a more authentic life. That's what happened for me when I allowed myself to freely use red and yellow on my personal canvas. Not only that, but it also allows us to be more open to change and opportunity. This is a big reason why the book in your hand is a mixture of those two colors– orange. The color of this book represents an authentic expression of who I am.

Nothing destroys dreams more than their creators. Not just achievement-based dreams, but dreams about the type of person we want to be. That's so, so dangerous because we are always one decision away from completely changing our lives. Limiting beliefs keep us from evolving and trans-forming ourselves and our lives. They might keep you from making that one decision that will positively impact you for the rest of your life.

Before we get into how to identify your limiting beliefs and how to rewrite them into something more empowering, let's have a quick discussion about why we create personal limiting beliefs in the first place.

We create limiting beliefs because we think they are serving us. They keep us safe and comfortable. We tell ourselves, "We're too dumb to try to apply for that scholarship," because we won't have to feel the sting of potential failure. We tell ourselves, "I'll never be in a healthy, long-term relationship," because it feels easier to give up rather than to keep trying. We tell ourselves, "It's Jeremy's fault we flopped during that presentation," because we're perfect, we don't make mistakes, and it couldn't possibly be *our* responsibility as well. We lie and lie and lie to ourselves because sometimes the truth is hard to swallow. I told myself I wasn't a loving person because it kept me safe from vulnerability, and I thought it helped me feel more at peace with how to label who I was.

We cling to limiting beliefs because change is uncomfortable. But by zooming out for a moment to see the big picture, our understanding of what is truly best for us shifts. When we step out of the circle that is our limiting belief, breaking the trap that holds ants (and us) captive, and charge into uncertainty and change, we are so much better in the long term.

How do we identify the need to venture out of our limiting circles and shift towards healthy change? And after that how do we avoid replacing an old confining circle with a new circle? Let's start with identifying and changing limiting beliefs, and then we'll wrap up with prevention moving forward.

Think for a moment, where do you hold yourself back? What negative things do you believe about yourself that you rarely give any room for fluidity or change? Write a few of those down.

Examples:

- I'm not smart enough
- I suck at talking to girls
- I'm too skinny
- I'm too fat
- Love is too painful
- If I act like the real me, people will hate it
- I don't deserve love
- Good things never come my way
- I always push people away

Now let's take a moment to rephrase those limiting beliefs into something more empowering. The starting point of changing our beliefs is reprogramming our self-talk.

A few rules of self-talk:

1. Avoid the terms "always" or "never." They are too rigid and lack fluidity.
2. Avoid using the phrase "I am" when referring to negative emotions, instead use the phrase "I feel."

Example of rephrased self-talk: "I **am always** anxious" can be rephrase to "I **feel** anxious **right now**, that's okay. I accept this feeling for what it is and when peace decides to return, I will welcome it."

Sounds super formal and weird, but it works y'all. It really works. I'd probably tell myself something more along the lines of, "Hmmm so I'm feeling anxious right now. Not loving that. Hey body, I'm listening. What's up? I hear you. Let it out, girl." I avoid spiraling into "WTF. I'm anxious all the time. Why!? I guess I'm just an anxious person and I always will be." The moment I decide that anxiety is what I am, I label myself as an anxiety-ridden person, the more I will manifest anxious feelings. Yes, I have been diagnosed with anxiety. I feel anxiety often, but I, myself, am not anxiety – anxiety is just something I feel. I am not anxious; I just feel anxious. The phrasing is key.

"I think therefore I am." You know that quote. It's so very true. Who you tell yourself you are or what you tell yourself you always do, matters. So, let's rephrase those limiting beliefs you have written down. How can we make them more compassionate and less rigid?

- I'm not smart enough to get into medical school. → Failure or struggle is not proof that I'm dumb. This is what I love, and I want to find a way to make it happen.
- I suck at talking to girls. → I am a person with a lot to offer, and I love having conversations with new people.
- I'm too fat to wear a crop top. → I'm so grateful for all my body does for me and my body is beautiful because it's mine. I give myself permission to fully express myself.
- Love is too painful. → I will no longer let pain hold me back from receiving love.
- If I act like the real me, people will hate it. → If I live authentically as myself, I will attract people doing the same. I don't need to be liked by *everyone*.
- I don't deserve love. → I am a person of worth. I am willing to receive love as often as I give it.
- I'm too skinny → Beauty is relative, and my body is art.
- Good things never come my way. → I have the capacity to identify opportunity when it presents itself.

- I always push people away. → I am someone that lets people in. I now know that vulnerability is a strength and a pathway to a happier life.

Yes, some of this rephrasing might feel like a total lie when you say it in your head. Doesn't matter. In my opinion, you're lying to yourself already, so might as well tell yourself a lie that serves you. The more you tell yourself that rephrased statement, the more you'll begin to believe it. Neurologically, your mind will begin to wire it into your mental recall as truth.

Self-talk, self-talk, self-talk, keep her under wraps. Stay very aware of what you let yourself think or say about who you are and what you do.

At the start of my career in becoming a twentysomething leader in the space of mindset, I constantly felt, and sometimes still do, totally unqualified. I finally sat myself down and said, "Livi, you telling yourself you're not qualified enough yet for x, y, and z is destroying your career growth."

Even though I didn't believe it at first, I started saying to myself, "People want to hear you and you deserve opportunities in this space." As soon as I stopped deciding I wasn't qualified enough for things, more opportunities started to open up. That same month that I decided I *was* qualified enough, I booked my first speaking gigs, had multiple podcast guest appearances, had my first literary agent show interest in my mission, booked podcast guests I thought would definitely reject me, and created my first speaker reel that I was actually proud of.

You are limitless. You are allowed to change. You are sublime.

Now decide that you are. No more lying. Throw those crusty, dusty, musty limiting beliefs in the trash.

# 9

# That Shit Hurted

**vul·ner·a·ble**
/ˈvəln(ə)rəb(ə)l/
adjective
**1. susceptible to physical or emotional attack or harm.**

Vulnerability. The mere mention of this word can make people squirm in their seats. Our subconscious minds sometimes associate our vulnerability with weakness, and it can definitely feel that way. We are a species that is ancestrally rooted in survival. Anytime we enter a territory where we're letting our guard down, our brain starts slamming the brake. Mental red lights are flashing saying "BAD, BAD, GO BACK, UNSAFE, SHUTTING DOWN." The trick of being a human is training our subconscious to be harmonious with our higher self. Our subconscious works to keep us safe (or what it thinks is safe), while our conscious mind keeps us authentically happy.

We live in a society that values confidence and "perfection" but doesn't seem to praise humility and authenticity as often. We seem to value vulnerability as individuals, though, so why do we undervalue it so much as a society? I believe much of this has to do with our struggle to value ourselves. Low self-worth usually stems from our parents, friends, or social media. As we compare ourselves to others and our abilities or qualities don't level up, we believe our value drops. With that, we set up walls to keep us safe. One of those defenses is not being vulnerable.

Allowing yourself to be vulnerable is a strength. It enables you to be your truest, most genuine self, and it also opens a safe place for others to do the same – have you ever noticed how we tend to admire when someone *else* knows how to be vulnerable? Being vulnerable is empowering because it allows you to get closer and closer to living in alignment. It allows for personal acceptance. Just like choosing love is a lot more courageous than choosing anger, choosing vulnerability is more courageous than always playing it safe.

One thing I find interesting about all this is that although our survivalist instincts tell us not to be vulnerable to survive, our brain also reminds us that we *need* other people to survive. We need a community to stay alive for food, protection, and reproduction. In the past, for our ancestors, banishment from a group, tribe, or community usually meant death. But how do we create a community of people? Connection. How do we create connections? Vulnerability.

## Let's Talk Healing

How do we allow ourselves to be vulnerable? We heal. We become harmonious with the pieces of us that weigh us down.

We are often told that time will heal all wounds. One thing I've learned about healing is that it's actually not time that brings it about –it's you. You bring about healing.

Although time contributes to healing all wounds; healing is extremely intentional.

What does it feel and look like when we become intentional about healing? When we believe it is time to hold our inner child's hand, time to love again, time to feel again, time to be ourselves again, or maybe even experience all that for the very first time. In all honesty... it sucks. That intentional healing hurts as much or more so than the experience that's brought us to this point itself, and it hurts like a mofo my friend. Well initially it doesn't suck because you're excited to move forward; then it sucks a whole lot; then it sucks so much your heart might explode; then your heart starts to fill with love. You see the greatness of the new you on the horizon, and you run to that person. You embrace that person, and then everything becomes still. It feels warm. You can breathe, and you allow yourself to do so. That's what healing feels like. It feels a lot, in fact, like . . . being vulnerable.

Healing is change, and it's the acceptance of change. In the process of healing, when it starts to hurt the most, that usually means you're onto something – you're feeling what is urging you to be felt. When you feel you heal, and suddenly greatness is on the horizon.

Now we know what healing looks like, what it feels like, and why the heck we do it – how do we heal? Let's navigate that process through a few concrete examples of trauma.

## The Healing Process: Moving from the Inner Circle to the Outer Circle

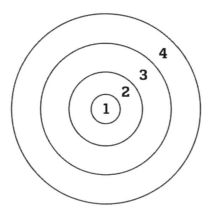

Damian grew up with a pretty emotionally abusive mom. She always told him he was a screw-up or that he needed to be more like his older brother. Damian rarely felt like his mom was proud of him and he wasn't even sure his mom loved him.

How does Damian *heal*? What does that journey look like?

### *1. Stage One: Awareness*

The awareness stage is coming to terms with the fact that something in your past is negatively affecting you. It could be affecting your productivity, your ability to fully feel emotions, your ability to stay calm during disagreements, your ability to trust others, your ability to receive or give love, your ability to receive physical touch, always feeling like you need to fix others or yourself, never feeling comfortable in your own body, feeling like everyone hates you, being afraid to speak your mind, feeling unworthy of success . . .

*Example*: Damian is now twenty-four years old and has entered a relationship with a really amazing guy named Elijah. Elijah is a walking green flag. Emotionally available, empathetic, honest, and doesn't struggle to express his love for Damian. This is something Damian isn't used to and is slowly becoming aware of his tendency to push Elijah away, not because he doesn't love him, but because Damian doesn't feel deserving of his love.

*Reminder*: Trauma, or experiences that require healing, can occur in a lot of ways. Even if you feel you didn't have anything particularly traumatic in your past, sometimes trauma is not what you experienced, sometimes it's what you didn't experience. For example, if your parents weren't aggressive or emotionally harmful, they were actually pretty good, but neither of them ever really expressed their emotions or made you feel like you could, that is something that can require a healing process, or more so, an emotional learning process. Nothing here was intentionally harmful, you just never learned how to express how you feel or that it was okay to do so.

### 2. Stage Two: Choosing Change

I've found that many people don't get past this stage until much later in life or never, which we want to try to avoid. The choosing change stage is deciding we *want* to put in some intentional work to feel more whole. *A lot of* people know they yell too much or know that they suck at forgiving others, or know that they often treat people poorly, but often, we decide it's "just the way we are," no change or growth is needed. Let me say now, most of the time change and growth *is* needed.

This stage is realizing something is causing an issue and needs to be worked through. We don't have to know how to do that or what exactly is causing the struggle yet, this stage is about awareness and a decision to change, no more avoidance. At this point, we have to let ourselves recognize that we feel unloved or angry or unfulfilled or sad or fearful or devastated and that's something we don't want to feel anymore. We want change and we are willing to make it happen.

*Example*: Damian really loves Elijah and wants to do whatever he can to improve his emotional availability to make the relationship better. Damian knows he doesn't want to push Elijah out of his life, so he decides that he's ready to commit to change and growth.

### 3. Stage Three: Feeling and Identifying

In stage three of the healing process we must do two things: allow ourselves to fully feel our painful emotions, as well as identify their source.

To heal, we have to allow ourselves to feel. Why is that? Our brains want to feel heard. When your brain is sending you anxious or fearful signals and emotions, it's trying to help you. It's trying to warn you or protect you. When Elijah tells Damian he loves him, Damian's mind has been wired by trauma to see this as danger. His brain sends a flight signal to keep him safe. If we never take a moment to tell our mind and body "Hey. I hear you. I hear you trying to keep me safe. Thank you," we will never work in harmony with our mind. Similar to a relationship conflict, most of the time we want to feel heard and understood first before conflict resolution, the same rule goes with you dealing with your brain's trauma triggers. Let your mind know that you hear her. Thank her for keeping you safe. If you don't acknowledge these emotional triggers that your mind is sending, it will keep sending them.

Chances are you've probably ignored or refused to accept these triggers your brain sends for years, let them finally flow and be felt like they've been wanting to after all this time. No more running, allowing ourselves to feel our emotions is not optional if we want to live a healthy life.

Along with feeling, in stage three we also are working on identifying the source of where these emotional triggers are coming from, why they were formed. Our neurological wiring is quite literally a record of our past. Who you are in this moment is because of the accumulation of all your past experiences, more on this in chapter twenty. If you are experiencing negative mental triggers in the present, your mind was wired to send those from something negative that happened in your past. We need to identify where in our past is affecting us. Identifying the source of our triggers will also help us understand if we need to forgive, remove, or speak with someone to move forward. It helps us become more self-aware, which makes moving forward a lot easier.

Instead of Damian saying, "Hey Brain! Stop making me pull away from my boyfriend, I love him," it makes much more sense and feels much more harmonious and healthier to say, "Hey Brain, I understand you're trying to keep me safe. I hear you. I know you are sending these signals because of how I grew up, but this is different. I'm safe here. Let's work on feeling safer here. Let's work on rewiring." The pieces add up in example two. There is much more compassion and understanding and we need to give that to ourselves.

Feeling and identifying are both in step three of healing because one person might be able to identify before they feel, someone else might work through this step by simultaneously feeling and trying to identify, it really depends on the individual and situation. What I find for me, because I tend to understand what trauma can cause specific triggers, I can usually identify in this stage pretty quickly. On the flip side, the feeling doesn't come as natural for me, having the analytical and "I am a fighter" mindset I have. I have to allow myself to feel, and that is usually when a lot of crying and talking happens, but it allows me to release what's been building up.

For someone else, feeling first and following that trail of emotions to find their source makes more sense. Again, very situational.

*Example*: Damian starts going to therapy and journaling. His therapists help him identify that his unlovable feelings stem from his childhood which helps him feel more empathetic and understanding of why he gets these feelings. Damian also uses journaling to finally allow himself to write down and feel all those hurt feelings he experienced growing up that he pushed deep down and kept locked up. Letting those emotions free finally allowed him to feel this deep unhappiness from his childhood start to fizzle away and not weigh him down. His brain is rewiring.

*Note*: It's so uncomfortable to heal because during that rewiring your physical body is also adjusting and is re-establishing its relationship with itself. Your brain is changing the way it's always functioned, that's uncomfortable for it. Your discomfort is not just emotional, it's neurological.

Different practices to help you feel and identify:

- Meditate (chapter eleven)
- Speak to a therapist (Keep in mind, it will most likely take some time to find a therapist that works for you.

Finding a therapist that you vibe with is a process that takes some patience and trial and error.)

- Journal (Prompt: What am I feeling in this moment? What feelings does this past experience bring up for me? What am I currently unwilling to feel?)
- Affirmations ("I am grateful for my past" or "My past is a piece of me but does not define me" or "My past will no longer confine me; I accept change into my life.")
- Read books surrounding the topic that you're working to heal (When I was working through my feelings surrounding love and relationships, I read books that addressed my struggles like *The Course of Love* and *The Mastery of Love*. Books like that helped me a lot. If you don't know someone that could recommend some book ideas for your healing process, all it takes is a Google search; "books about love," "books about healing," "top books about grieving," "forgiveness book" – it could be one of the best Google searches you ever do. I also have book recs on my website, liviredden.com/resources & I post them a lot on Instagram, @liviredden)

### 4. Step Four: Self-Empowerment

Now that you've become aware of your pain, chosen change, allowed yourself to feel, and identified the source of your emotional pain, it's time to let the new version of you emerge. Here we fully accept our past for what it is, learn from it, and have reached a mentally rewired state. We aren't forgetting our past, it's still part of you, it just no longer constrains you. It also is no longer used as a crutch for behavior that is unloving towards us and others. Your past no longer controls your future. You have stepped into a new chapter.

How do we know when we've healed or become self-empowered? Easiest way put: you no longer have an intense physical reaction. You'll no longer get a rock in your stomach when you explain your past. Your shoulders won't tighten up when you see that person that caused you pain. A rush of anxiety won't overtake you anytime something triggers that piece of your past.

You also will have a healthier internal narrative; chapter eight can be highly ingrained into a healing process. *That's* how you know you've healed.

You must know, healing is often never quite complete. We might feel pretty healed in the moment and five years down the line something rips back open that wound and we're back in therapy. We're journaling or meditating on it again. That's normal.

Healing is work. If you want to heal, it takes work. Only you can decide that it's time to heal. Only you can decide you refuse to let your past continue to hinder your future. Only you can decide to hold hands with your pain, feel it, learn from it, thank it for its teaching, and take the next step into the unrestrained version of you. You decide. We attract what we desire. When we desire to heal, we attract it, but we must decide if we embrace it and take action when we attract opportunities to heal.

Once we heal ourselves it allows us to love more freely. To exist more freely. To connect. To be vulnerable. To experience joy. That is the power of healing.

Here's the last thing I want to mention about healing from our past.

A lot of this trauma and unhealthy mental processes that we're trying to heal or change or unlearn was unprovoked. Most of us at this stage in life find our pain or poor mindset rooted in our childhood or young adulthood. Much of this healing we have to do was caused by someone who decided not to heal. It's unfair. And I recognize the shitty reality of that.

You didn't wake up one morning and say, "You know what I could use: more PTSD and heartbreak." You didn't sit on Santa's lap as an eight-year-old and say "Santa, this year I'd love a puppy, a tie-dye kit, and divorced parents."

But the thing is, although we don't get to choose our pain, it is our choice whether or not to continue to suffer.

The harsh reality of taking ownership over our process of becoming the 2.0 aligned & healed version of ourselves is that if you don't do it – no one is coming to save you.

No one is coming to save you.

It is your responsibility and your responsibility alone to get onto the driver's seat of your life. There is no upgrade to a self-driving car. We either learn how to drive or we will eventually crash. Mentors can provide some GPS. Loved ones can give you someone to chat with or harmonize to Queen with, but the steering wheel can only be directed by you.

You have to choose to confront yourself.

To tell that voice in your head that says you're too screwed up, you're too unlovable, you're not enough that you are choosing to intentionally take control now. Tell that voice you know you have potential and you're about to reach it.

Once we decide we have limitless potential, it gives us limitless potential.

And tapping into that potential starts in the being. In the healing. In the unlearning and the rewiring. Recognizing that this attachment we might have to victimhood and our struggle, and the drama is not serving us. Not if you want to be better. Not if you want your pain and past to no longer have power over you.

Allow yourself to be vulnerable again through the power of healing so you can more fully experience the joy this life has to offer.

If you make one life-altering decision today, this week, this year:

**Choose to heal.**

# 10

# The Girl Who Cried Lion

Two words: Headrest TV. If your childhood consisted of this seemingly lovely invention and it brings back fond memories of family, road trips, and watching Lightning McQueen miss winning the Piston Cup in an act of empathy and love, I'm happy for you. Now if you didn't have a DVD Player strapped to the back of a parent or guardian's headrest growing up, I'm here to tell you, you missed nothing. I said this invention is "seemingly lovely" for a reason – truly it's a gateway to years of night sweats and sleepwalking. This is my extreme way of telling you that this invention was the source of unlocking my biggest childhood fear: Lions.

Around the age of eight, I was sitting in the back of our silver Nissan with my sister, eating my road trip treat of choice, a long, yellow, banana Laffy Taffy. We had probably just finished watching *Hairspray* for the twentieth time and my Dad returned from the gas station Redbox with his movie of choice, *Prey*. He popped it into our headrest TVs and exclaimed "I've been waiting to watch this one, let me know what you guys think." Why my Dad felt he had the exact same taste in movies as his eight-year-old daughter and was asking for her feedback, I have no idea. How my mom, the woman that didn't even like me watching *The Incredible Hulk* at that age, didn't notice this rated-R thriller being placed into our screens, I also have no idea. There I sat in my SpongeBob t-shirt with my stuffed giraffe in hand. My eyes are fixated upon my father's movie selection; watching a group of stranded Safari tourists getting ripped apart on a Jeep windshield by lion fang's bigger than my forearms. My childhood fear had officially been: Unlocked.

From that day on I became less of a fan of the zoo and even less of a fan of the movie *Life of Pi* that came out four years later. In *Life of Pi*, it's a tiger, but regardless, any big cats had become a giant no from me. Why that fear lasted so long, I couldn't tell you. Especially considering we lived in the suburbs of Utah with absolutely no threat of lions coming to eat my face off. One thing I do remember from the years of lion-based nightmares was how my mom's patience and love for me were truly tested.  Shout out to Mama Leah for passing that test with flying colors.  I remember my mom always being accepting and empathetic when I showed up in her doorway at three in the morning (like that "I threw up" meme) once again explaining that I had woken up to a dream about a lion coming out of my closet and ripping off my limbs. Not once do I remember my mom getting angry with me or telling me that I just needed to stop being scared. She would hug me, sing songs with me, sleep next to me, kindly talk to me about whether or not lions really were an immediate threat. Bless that woman's heart considering from an adult's perspective this fear was absolutely ridiculous. She was able to access empathy for me in those moments almost every time I woke her up from the bliss of deep sleep and I think that's a beautiful thing we can all learn from.

As an adult, I've asked my mom why she was so patient with me through years and years of nightmares and night sweats. She said it was two things that allowed her to access empathy at 3 AM, multiple times a week: gratitude and remembering her own childhood. She would see me in the doorway and think about how much she loved being a mom, especially since the medical road to popping out two kids of her own took just under ten years and was far from easy. My mom would also access empathy by thinking of herself as a little girl. She told me, as a child, she would have nightmares, too. She'd wake up terrified and waddle down the hallway to *her* mom, who was almost always awake it seemed, and was probably up doing laundry for their low-income family of twelve. Her mom was always so loving and gentle with her in those moments, regardless of how tired she undoubtedly was. My mom told me that when she was a girl, she couldn't make it through the night at any sleepover. She'd get too scared. Because of those experiences in her own childhood, when I showed up panicking about another lion nightmare, my mom would recall her own memories. She knew what it felt like to be that scared little girl at their mom's bedside.

That empathy in my childhood was the foundation of my trust in my mom in high school, college, and now. I knew she would always try to empathize with me no matter what crap I'd done or said. Accessing empathy when it is the hardest is one of the purest actions of love we can take.

## What Is Empathy, How Do We Build It, and Why Do We Need to Work on It?

Empathy is key to a happy life and growing into our most ethereal selves. Empathy for others and empathy for ourselves is how we let love in when we need it most.

Empathy is defined as "the action of understanding, being aware of, being sensitive to, and vicariously experiencing the feelings, thoughts, and experience of another of either the past or present without having the feelings, thoughts, and experience fully communicated in an objectively explicit manner."

Empathy is feeling WITH someone. Empathy is using what you know about pain, fear, and shame to put yourself in someone else's situation by considering their perspective, background, limitations, and values. There is a video from years ago on YouTube that describes what empathy looks like  and what makes it different from sympathy. Scan this code to watch or google "Brené Brown on Empathy."

Empathy is choosing to take a ladder and enter a dark hole that someone else is in and feel the reality of that darkness with them as best you can. Sympathy is chucking a sandwich and some crossword puzzles into that hole and wishing them the best.

If you are currently trying to or are having a hard time accessing empathy for someone you love, here are a few things that might help.

### 1. Take Mental Wiring into Account

Whether we are trying to heal, to be a loving support system, or trying to let go of angry feelings, here is an idea that might be worth thinking about. To access empathy, we must understand that the person we are trying to empathize with could have a completely different set of wiring than the one we have. Biologically speaking, this person may not be wired the way you are. They simply cannot access the logic or way of being that you can access. This difference in wiring may have to do with mental illness or different neurological development before birth. This person could be playing with a *very* different neurological hand than you.

Taking someone else's biological limitations into account has allowed me to more quickly access forgiveness, understanding, and love. It helps to give me the ability to move forward when someone else has wronged me. As people, our bodies and minds are imperfect and not everyone has the same capabilities that you have. Some people physically can't access the ability to show love the way that you can or be nurturing in the way that you can. They are not able to show emotional support the way you can, move on from their past the way you can, or access drive and ambition the way that you can. Some brains just simply do not function like yours. Therefore, with the neurological wiring and mental functions they were born with, they truly can't access certain pieces of the brain that you can and are simply doing their best with the biology they received at birth and so are you.

Our neurological systems are so advanced that we don't fully understand the power or limitations our brains possess. I've discovered that for me, deciding to chalk someone's bad behavior towards me or confusing sadness or anger to their mental wiring can help, and sometimes we need others to do the same for us. We might not have the mental capabilities somebody else has. I decide to land on that sometimes just for my own sanity and to let go of my confusion or sadness or anger and truly stop caring if I'm right or wrong. If it helps me heal and feel a restored sense of love, peace or allows me to be a better support system for someone I love, so be it.

## 2. What Information Are You Missing About This Person's Past?

How did this particular person grow up? How might their upbringing affect the way they are acting or reacting? Could this be a trauma response manifesting? Our past creates the wiring for how our brain currently functions. If someone hasn't had external support or exposure to wellness concepts, they would need to go through the process of rewiring their brain from the unhealthy patterns programmed into them from the past. Sometimes all we can do is be patient with them.

Have you ever asked this person about their past? What has this person gone through that you know nothing about? What is this person currently going through? If you don't know, you should probably ask before you judge. If we have decided we want to access more empathy for a particular person we can't just put ourselves in their current situation, we can improve understanding if we also take into account what it would feel and look like to walk their path, to walk their past.

## 3. Have I Experienced a Pain Like the One Being Described to Me?

Now, this isn't about explaining to someone that you know exactly how they feel because you experienced X, Y, & Z. This is about recalling your emotions from one of your personal past experiences that could be relatively similar to what this person you love is going through.

*Example*: Say a friend of yours just broke up with their partner. You've never been through a breakup so you're not sure how to be there for them. You think about what you've experienced that might be similar. You haven't been through a romantic breakup, but you recall the feelings you had when you had to break off a friendship with a long-time close friend. You remember just wanting someone to give you a hug and listen. Recalling those emotions of your own, silently in your mind, at that moment can help you better support your friend that's struggling. Seems really simple, but many people struggle to do this. To access true empathy. We might just think, "Oh, that's sad," and not take a moment to really think about what they're feeling. In our toughest moments, we want to feel understood and if you want to provide that understanding for someone else, it requires empathy.

Now let's talk about self-empathy. As important as it is for us to have empathy for others, it is even more important we practice empathy with ourselves. It is important we balance our desire to grow and do our best, alongside healthy doses of, acceptance of our failures or personal forgiveness for regrettable events in our past.

If you are currently trying to increase the empathy you give yourself, try these steps.

## 1. What Did You Not Know?

I remember recently recalling a specific experience from my past that had me feeling extremely shameful. I started to talk to a friend about it and how embarrassed and lame it made me feel. After expressing my emotions, she asked me, "How old were you when that happened?" I told her that I was fourteen at the time. After talking with her, I realized I was feeling shame about something I'd done years and years prior. I was fourteen, I needed to cut myself some slack. I was literally a child. I'm hardly even the same person anymore, I barely knew half of what I know now.

When you look back at your past and begin to feel shame, stress, or anxiety, ask yourself, "What did that version of me not know yet?" That version of you was different from the current you. Sometimes we just need to cut ourselves some slack and stop feeling shame for the things we did that helped us learn the hard way.

## 2. What Was Your Intention?

Sometimes our intent was WAY better than the actual result or action. I'm a believer that the desire of your heart truly matters. You know yourself. You know whether or not your intention was pure and that matters when accessing personal empathy. Sometimes we might have a desire to feel love and we do something out of character to try to get that. Sometimes we might have a desire to help someone, and it ends up making things worse for them. Give yourself some empathy if the result didn't quite match up with your good intention. It happens.

## 3. Am I Growing as a Person Even Though I Experience Setbacks?

Again, cut yourself some slack for the screw-ups. If your general projection is growth and improvement as a person, that is something to celebrate. Sometimes the lows are super, super low and that's okay. Sometimes we take one step forward and 5 steps back in our personal growth, but we still move one step forward. Be proud of yourself for that one step. The growth process is not perfectly linear.

### 4. If You Learned From Your Past, Guilt Is No Longer Necessary!

We beat ourselves up over and over and over and over again about moments in our past. I'm looking at my dog, Koda, as I write this and I'm pretty sure he doesn't do that. He lives in the present for the most part it seems. Ya, he may have gotten into trouble for eating a sock or peeing on the carpet in the past, but he doesn't replay it over and over in his mind and let that shame drag him down. He is just full of love and joy for others and himself in this moment. He's present. We don't need to punish ourselves a million times because of one screw-up. Take the time to right your wrongs and learn from them. STOP RELIVING THEM. It's not serving you. Just decide that today will be better. Decide to remember and act on the lesson you learned and how you've changed. Stop the punishing acts that are shattering you every time you finish picking up the pieces.

Affirmation for your week: I am at peace with my past, present, and future.

Look at yourself with eyes of empathy every day this week and say this mantra to yourself in the mirror. Let empathy heal you. No more shame and guilt. You deserve to heal and shed the old version of yourself. That version of you that did that thing that you wish every day you hadn't done doesn't even exist anymore. You're a different person now, allow yourself to move forward and be in the present moment. Please stop letting your shame, and guilt tear you apart like the way those lions tore those people apart in *Prey*. Allow yourself to move forward without all the self-loathing and resentment.

Choose empathy.

# 11

# Why Meditation Isn't Just for Moms & Monks

**"Have the courage to sit soberly in your reality."**
**— Elizabeth Gilbert**

When I first heard about the idea of daily meditation, my initial reaction was as follows:

1. I can't sit still that long.
2. Sounds super boring.
3. Isn't that just for monks and middle-aged moms?

Now I've been practicing meditation for more than five years, and daily meditation for more than three (my consistency with it has, of course, had its ups and downs). I can tell you that all three of these common reactions are false. You most likely *can* sit still that long. It *isn't* boring. Meditation is for *everyone*.

By the way, If you don't prefer the word *meditation*, you can also replace it with the word stillness or moments of little to no external input. That's all it is.

If you do one, just *one,* exercise I share with you in this book, choose meditation. Meditation has changed my life, the lives of millions, and *I guarantee* it can change yours.

Before I get into what meditation is and how to do it, I'll first tell you what it isn't.

Meditation is not:

- Just for spiritual people.
- Thinking about nothing.
- A practice that looks the same for everyone.

Recently, I've started doing my first speaking gigs about emotional intelligence, mindfulness, and mindset. I've learned that a good public speaker conveys their personal story in a way that doesn't make them the main character; it makes their listeners the main character. You want the audience to see themselves in your story. For example, the rags to riches trope. Society doesn't love that type of story because of the person that is gaining riches, but because they see themselves as someone who is on their personal rags-to-riches journey – it provides hope. The story is relatable enough that we can place ourselves into that plotline. We can make ourselves the hero.

First, I had to narrow in on what my story was and how I wanted to share it. To learn how to do that, I took a four-week course that allowed me to tell my story about why I do what I do professionally in just two minutes. The course helped me answer the question: what in my past made me so passionate about what I do today? The two-minute blurb I con-structed has helped me immensely when it comes to public speaking. A key I was taught in delivering that two-minute piece was to not get overwhelmed by telling it word for word every time. A course mentor told me, "At the end of the day, you know your story. Speak from your heart and not just your brain." I love that. My ability to connect with an audience heavily lies in my ability to speak from the heart. To let my heart guide me. To trust myself. That is also how I've tried to write this book – from the heart.

This mindset of trusting our heart and intuition relates to a lot of areas of our life. The answers you seek are not outside of you, but inside. All our hearts and minds ask is that we listen and trust them. How do we do this?

Every big decision I've made in the past few years was mainly based on conversations with my higher self during meditation. Asking myself how she feels and what she thinks is the most aligned for Livi. I have those conversations via meditation.

These were some of the questions I used meditation to find answers to:

- Whether to move to San Diego from Utah
- Which business idea I should focus on for maximum fulfillment and joy
- Whether I should drop out of college and lose my full-ride scholarship
- Whether I should keep certain people in my life

Three out of four of these questions I would have answered differently had I not meditated on it. I would have initially taken a very different path, just listening to my logical brain. But I meditated, leaned on the trust I've built with myself, and feel the happiest and most aligned I've ever been.

I want to focus on the question about my business. I had to decide between two business ventures – starting a podcast production company or contracting my writing and marketing skills to business coaches. My initial plan was to pursue the podcast company. I typed up a business plan. I had my logo, my marketing plan, my hiring plan, my potential client list, my website layout plan, and my company name ready to roll. Before I started to execute, I finally paused for a moment and asked myself, "Livi, is this aligned with you? Is this what you really want? Remember the goal is to live in alignment."

The next morning, I meditated on it, hoping my heart and mind (and God, as meditation is also a spiritual practice for me) would tell me I should continue with the podcast company. Long story short, that is not the answer I got. I was so very irritated. I'd already done all the work. Plus, I would most likely hit six figures for myself in just one year with the podcast business idea. Frustrated, I meditated on it again. Should I start the podcast company? The same frustrating answer, no. It *must* be a mistake, I thought. Soooo, the next day, I meditated even longer. Podcast company or freelance work with coaches? Same answer, no to the podcast company.

Let me expound on what I mean when I say the "answer I got was *no*." What does it mean to receive an answer during meditation? Answers that are coming from the deepest, truest parts of you are usually a feeling or a nudge more than they are words or thoughts.

The amazing thing about meditation is that when you go into it focusing on a specific question, you can receive answers to those questions without actively thinking or brainstorming answers. All you're doing is creating a clearing. When I tell you "the answers are usually already inside you," I mean that sometimes you just need to give yourself the stillness and the silence to let your mind, body, and spirit give you that answer.

Meditation gives you a moment to stop looking externally for an answer and to look internally for what you should do next. That's what "receiving" an answer looks like for me.

I did in fact shut down the podcast, throwing a white surrender flag in the air and tossing the idea in the trash. I let my intuition win, and you know what? She was right. SHE WAS FREAKING RIGHT. Of course, she was right. I went with doing freelance work. I made way less money, but I was happier, more fulfilled, and the skills and connections I made will monetize forever. Meditating for thirty to sixty minutes over a three-day period allowed me a happier life for the next few years of my career. What a blessing. If that doesn't convince you to have a budding interest in meditation, I don't know what will.

Now for . . .

# MEDIATION 101

## Step One - What is Meditation?

First, I want to help you understand what meditation is. Meditation is about creating a still space for yourself that allows you to gain clarity.

> **"Stillness is not about focusing on nothingness; it's about creating a clearing. It's opening up an emotionally clutter-free space and allowing ourselves to feel and think and dream and question."**
> **— Brene Brown**

Many people live their lives on autopilot. We wake up, go to work or school, get home, fill any free moment with activities, our phones, or other people, and then we go to sleep. Not a single moment of stillness, only external stimulation. Meditation is about creating just a few moments of stillness to break that autopilot cycle. Stillness, not nothingness.

Why does breaking the autopilot cycle matter? Because you can't live in alignment if you just follow the herd, you need to create a moment to listen to yourself. To listen to the answers that are already inside of you. If we never listen to what our heart is trying to tell us, we'll spend our lives doing what we think we should do, what everyone else is doing, or what everyone is telling us we should do. Autopilot will leave you on your deathbed with regrets, pits of unfulfilled dreams, and wishing you'd experienced more joy. That's dark, but that's what autopilot, zombie-mode does to people. Not that you'll die with a terrible life, but you'll miss out on what life could have been like at its best.

To tie it in a bow, the first thing to remember about meditation: the goal is not nothingness, but stillness for the sake of additional clarity. You don't have to clear your mind during meditation. It's about allowing your subconscious thoughts to become conscious. To give your body and mind a moment of stillness to communicate with you. Sinking into a level of consciousness and presence.

The second thing to understand, this moment of stillness won't always be peaceful. Many times, it sucks. A million things you've been pushing down come bubbling up. You get answers you don't want. You cry. You feel frustrated. Sitting soberly and calmly in your emotions and internal conflicts is a hard thing. Teaching your body that it's okay to be still after years of constant stimulation is tough. We are addicted to being constantly entertained and stimulated. Addicted. When you start meditating, you are breaking an addiction. It's not easy, but you know, and I know, that addiction or too much of anything is bad, obviously. Meditation will help you slowly wean your way off autopilot day by day.

The third thing you must learn, or unlearn, to start practicing meditation is how answers to the tough questions actually come to us. How do you usually figure out the answer to something? You probably said by thinking. That's usually not the case when it comes to answering life-related questions, though. You get answers by not thinking. I'm not crazy, hear me out.

It seems counterintuitive, right? Not thinking to get an answer or idea, but it works. Why? Because the answers we search for about our lives usually lie within us, not outside of us. When you create a still space for clarity, you are peacefully letting your inner voice, your subconscious, your higher self, the Universe, God, and/or whoever bring answers to you instead of always chasing after them. Sometimes during meditation, you receive answers or advice without even asking a question. Your soul just sends you a burst of intuition like, "Hey buddy, have this, thanks for taking the time to tune in." So cool! Then all you have to do is follow those bursts of intuition, that is a core principle of living in alignment. Accepting and taking action towards what your soul is naturally nudging you towards.

## Step Two - How to Meditate

There is no one correct way to meditate. It's something you get to customize to who you are. The goal is to get to a meditative, still state. How you get there is somewhat irrelevant.

A list of meditative variations (I'll leave these for you to Google if you'd like):

- Guided Meditation - listening to a prerecorded or live meditation and having it guide you into a meditative state, great for beginners, available on apps like Calm or on YouTube
- Mantra Meditation - repeating and focusing on specific words or sounds to enter a meditative state, great for manifesting or healing
- Movement Meditation - yoga is a great example of this, great for those with very overactive minds, helps you to let your mind and body to work more in harmony
- Transcendental Meditation - a form of mantra meditation created by Indian guru, Maharishi Mahesh Yogi, that is geared towards more serious meditators,

generally, your mantra is given to you by a teacher or guru, great for more experienced meditators. If you want to learn this, I would seek out a teacher online or in person

- Spiritual or Prayer-based Meditation - praying while in a meditative state and is used to connect with God(s) or the Universe, great for spiritual individuals
- + Many, Many More

I've practiced all five forms I mentioned above, but generally, I focus on spiritual and Transcendental meditation. Meditation is BOMB! It helps me physically, mentally spiritually, and has also been so great as I've learned to work with my anxiety.

I want you to walk away from this chapter with a few meditation techniques and to understand the basic steps to entering a meditative state.

## The Basics

Here is a very basic step-by-step to meditation, but again, there isn't really a wrong way to meditate:

1. Go to a shaded area outside or slightly dim the lights of a private, quiet room.
2. Sit down with your legs crossed. If that's uncomfortable you can also have your back against a wall with your legs out, or you can sit in a chair with your feet firmly on the floor . . . again, no wrong way to do it. Just be comfortable.
3. Set a timer for 5-20 minutes (there are great meditation timer apps that will ease you out of your

meditation with calm sounds instead of a scary, jolting phone alarm. I used my phone alarm for a while in my meditation journey and no matter how much I turned my phone volume down, it would scare the shit out of me every time. I do not recommend it.)

4. Close your eyes (preferred) or focus on one specific object in front of you.

5. Place your hands in your lap or on your knees, palms facing up (palms up helps with openness and a willingness to receive) or hands together (to balance your energies).

6. Listen to a guided meditation or a specific musical frequency (ex. 852 Hz is considered a frequency that will increase your intuitive instincts in life and love. You can find hour-long versions of these on Spotify or YouTube). I wouldn't recommend a meditation playlist, because it will bounce around to different songs with different moods which throws your concentration off. You can also just sit in silence, but I wouldn't recommend this for a beginner. Note: If I'm listening to something, I prefer headphones. It's much more immersive and helps me slip into a meditative state faster.

7. Take some very deep and long breaths to calm your body and mind (deep inhale, long exhale).

8. Continue to take deep breaths and let your breath slowly return to its natural rhythm. Focus on your breath, let it be your anchor to the present moment. Let your body really focus on the pleasure of feeling your lungs with air. Breathing in your source of life. If thoughts start popping up, don't try to stop them.

Let them flow in and out of your brain. Imagine a freeway on a TV screen, occasional cars zooming back and forth, those cars are your thoughts. Let your thoughts pop onto the screen and drive past, not paying them too much mind. You can also think of your thoughts as clouds passing by. You are becoming the observer of your thoughts. If more thoughts keep coming up, just do your best to bring your attention back to your breath. Focus on that anchor.

9.  Here you can just follow your meditation guide OR if you are self-guiding, I've included some techniques below that you can include to mix things up rather than just focusing on your breath the whole time, which you can also do if you'd prefer. These techniques can add variety and depth to your meditative practice.

If it's a short meditation, only do one technique per session. These are all techniques I've used or currently use.

**Breathing Circle**: Imagine a circle in your mind. As you breathe, watch that circle expand. As you exhale, watch the circle shrink. Let that circle be an imaginative, physical addition to your anchor aka your breath. Stay deeply focused on that circle.

**Body Scanning**: Bring your attention to your toes and slowly move up your body to your feet, your legs, your stomach, your chest, your shoulders, until you reach the top of your head. Notice where you feel aches or pain, send positive thoughts and energy to those areas of your body. Notice where you are tense, allow those areas to relax. Drop your shoulders, unclench your jaw . . . I've experienced firsthand that this technique can give you a lot or complete pain relief. Very cool.

**Movement**: One movement I do in almost every meditation is to relieve shoulder tightness. I work on the computer a lot, on top of life stresses, I hold a lot of tension in my shoulders and neck. As you breathe slowly, tilt your head to your right. Let all or most of your head's weight stretch out the muscles in the left side of your shoulder and neck. Let those muscles release. Now do the same, tilting your head to the left and releasing your right side. I notice vast differences in my neck and shoulder muscle tenseness when I'm doing or not doing this exercise. This one is a game-changer.

**Mantras/Affirmations**: Repeat short phrases slowly in your mind or out loud throughout your meditation. You can come up with your own phrase, and I would actually recommend that, but here are some examples if you'd like – "I'm enough and I matter," "I am at peace with my past, present, and future," "Fear and pain does not hold me back from receiving love," "I live in a state of flow," or "I am whole and I am present."

**Visualizations**: Let your mind select a word that you want to attract more of into your life. Love, peace, patience, opportunity, whatever comes to mind that you need more of. Imagine that word written out in your mind and focus on it, you can slowly repeat it in your mind if you'd like. Now imagine a stream of soft light or glowing sand entering your palms and dispersing through your body, kind of like Rapunzel's hair in *Tangled*. You can also imagine that light entering your feet, dispersing throughout your body, and exiting through the top of your head out into the Universe, and then returning back to your feet, like a massive circle of light that extends to the sky and is running through your body. As you imagine this, know that the light and energy you are receiving from the Universe is the one word you are focused on. You are letting the Universe supply you with that one word you need more of. More Love. More Peace. More Opportunity. You are connecting with the Universe and letting her offer you the energy you seek.

Can't say enough times that I urge you to put meditation into practice. You could start by doing it just once per week. You could do just five minutes every day in the morning after you brush your teeth or make your bed. Meditation will supply you with so much clarity, presence, and peace. Your mind is so much more powerful than you might think, let yourself unlock that power.

# 12

# The Honesty Policy

I want to introduce and tell you a little about my Aunt Mo to kick off this chapter. I'll start by describing her house. This house could be described as colorful, organized chaos. This woman is a vintage and DIY queen. She has old-fashioned magazines and newspapers mod-podged to cover her countertops. She has vintage displays throughout the house by category: Asian art style inspired, western, rooster themed, monochromatic, etc. Homemade collages, shadow boxes, and paintings on every wall. A plethora of vintage knick knacks, clothing items, suitcases, pillowcases, hand towels, pictures, craft supplies, toys, silverware, books, games, aprons – the list could go on.

Every area of the house has some sort of "Aunt Mo" touch to it. It's honestly amazing, it's like walking through an antique mall. If I was at that house during the 2020 coronavirus quarantine, it would probably take weeks for me to get bored. If you're a fan of thrifting and are ever in Washington state, my Aunt Mo could give you the guide to all the best places for thrifting success. What's even better than her passion for vintage is her kindness and acceptance of others. She has a gift for making everyone in her life, including strangers, feel loved and accepted in her presence. Truly a special woman. There are only a handful of people in my life who can get me crying on the floor laughing and I could go to for advice and feel safe being in an emotional vulnerable state. My Aunt Mo is one of those people. I also know that she is someone who will be completely honest with me, even if it's something that isn't easy to hear.

One instance in particular was when me and her were in the Taco Bell drive thru. I'd been talking to my therapist at that time about getting a better understanding of my family members' personalities. I was talking to Aunt Mo about how I was feeling about it and the things I'd learned. She was discussing some of the tendencies she had seen in my family and a few bits of advice on how I could better understand them from her point of view. I then asked her, "What is something you see in my personality that I could improve or work on." She seemed hesitant to answer my question, but I think she knew I genuinely wanted her opinion, regardless of how it made me feel. She turned to me and said, "You aren't very quick to help." I looked at her a bit puzzled and asked her to explain a little more. She relayed an experience that explained what she meant.

My Dad was diagnosed with ALS, a terminal illness, when I was eleven. This disease has no treatment or cure. My Dad wasn't the type to sit on the sidelines and he always worked hard for what he believed in. My Dad refused to go down in silence. That is how the Kickin' ALS 5k races came about. Friends, family, and neighbors rallied around us to help us pull these races off year after year. Our third and last race we hosted was a bit of a struggle.

We were short on volunteers and time.

My Aunt Mo knew how much this race meant to my Dad and flew to Utah to help coordinate and drive people to make this thing happen. The day of the race everyone was up early and frantically working on last-minute preparation. If only I could say the same for myself. My Aunt Mo recalled that in the early morning of preparing for that race I was still asleep in bed. I showed up to the preparation party probably two hours later than a lot of the other volunteers when it was a race for my own Dad.

Still sitting in the Taco Bell parking lot, I realized she was completely right. I sat there thinking to myself, "Are you kidding me?! All these people were there helping your family. You are claiming to be grateful for all these people, but you had the audacity to *sleep* while they worked. Definitely not okay." I will say, I also considered the fact that this story she told me was four years prior. I was nineteen when this conversation about my fifteen-year-old behavior had occurred, but I felt that it still rang true and was something I could probably work on. Since I was a kid, for one reason or another, jumping up and helping wasn't habitual. Still writing that down makes me sick to my stomach and slightly ashamed. I was quick to help when I wanted to, but if my assistance wasn't a necessity, there was usually some lag in my participation. I often wasn't the first to go help someone with their luggage or clear off the dinner table. But I've accepted this, and I know flaws come with being human. All I can do is improve and show myself grace.

I told my Aunt that what she told me was completely true. I am so grateful for my Aunt's honesty at that moment. She was willing to tell me something I might not have liked hearing but needed to. If she hadn't told me that, I may not have ever consciously made the changes necessary to be more of a person who jumps up and helps. I've definitely made big improvements since then and try my best to make conscious efforts to be of assistance to others. I was on a linear progression as I can see this skill had vastly improved between the two stories, but her bringing it to my attention allowed it to be something I could consciously work on to allow for more of an exponential progression.

The lesson here: The courage to be fully honest with others, even when it isn't easy, matters.

Now, I want to make the distinction between being fully honest and being brutally honest. To me, being fully honest comes from a place of kindness and having someone's best interest in mind, like the story I shared above. Being brutally honest often comes from a place of anger, sadness, or insecurity. It's usually unnecessary. There is a quote that was shared with me that basically says, those who take pride or boast about being "brutally honest," usually seem to enjoy the "brutal" part more than the "honest" part. It's an act of selfishness, not selflessness. Before we open our mouths to deliver honestly, we need to ask ourselves, "What's my motive here? Does this *actually* need to be said?" For example, if someone laughs really awkwardly or loudly, we don't need to point it out. All it will do is cause insecurity and possibly make that person suppress a piece of themselves that is used to express their joy, and that is a terrible thing.

Not only can being honest with those we love and being accepting of honest feedback help us and others as individuals, but it can help create healthier relationships and prevent a lot of pent-up resentment.

When my sister, Lexi, and her boyfriend had been dating for about six months, he told my sister that our family had some issues with interrupting. The next time my sister was with my mom and I, she told us what her boyfriend had said. We discussed it and realized that we all really did have a problem with interrupting when others were talking, mainly within our own family.

Growing up my mom, sister, and I talked a lot. We talked about our emotions, daily life, school, dating, you name it. We talked about everything together. In doing so we found all of our mental processing styles were very out loud; it's the best way we think through things. For so long, when we would all talk, if a thought or additional comment came to our head, we would say it while the other was talking. The person talking would acknowledge and keep going, so within our family, it became normal to us. We'd never been told or even thought about doing things otherwise. We saw it as the other person simply adding a comment. We didn't see it as disrespectful. This habit was something that bothered Lexi's boyfriend and made him feel like what he had to say was unimportant when he talked to one of us. After my sister told us about our family's interrupting habit, the three of us made a conscious effort to break it. Since then our communication skills have improved a lot within our family. I'm grateful that her boyfriend said something, as we may have never noticed otherwise.

The lesson here: The courage to be fully honest with others, even when it isn't easy, is very important, especially to keep any type of relationship healthy. Aside from asking yourself whether a specific comment is actually necessary, as I mentioned earlier, also ask yourself: Is this someone who will be receptive to my loving honesty? If they don't like what I feel I should tell them, what will the result be within this relationship? When we are honest with others and express how we feel, we are showing ourselves and others love. We are practicing healthy relationship habits.

Being honest with yourself is the root of emotional awareness and learning self-love. When we are honest with ourselves about our strengths and weaknesses, we are doing three things:

1. Building trust with ourselves
2. Learning to be at peace with our imperfections
3. Building foundations for future and current relationships

## Building Trust Within Ourselves

When we consistently show ourselves that we know how to assess with reason and practicality where we are doing well and where we are not, we train our brains to trust us. To trust that we will take in information and process information with reason rather than reaction. We gain confidence in our ability to love ourselves for our good qualities, while still acknowledging and growing with our flaws. When we trust ourselves with our own thought processes and perceptions, we will also build trust in taking in outside information with self-kindness, self-awareness, and neutrality.

## Learning to Be at Peace with Our Imperfections

I believe that self-honesty is one of the roots of self-love. It allows you to be at peace with your imperfections. It is the first step of growth. Although, there is no step-by-step instruction manual on learning self-honesty, when you find yourself being dishonest or overly hard on yourself, start by frequently asking yourself these questions:

1. Am I validating my own feelings right now?
2. Am I allowing myself to feel my emotions at this moment?
3. Is what I'm saying to myself in fairness and neutrality?
4. Am I being dishonest with myself in some of these statements I'm making in my mind?
5. What do I truly need to do or NOT do to recognize and dissolve this frustration, anxiety, sadness, or self-loathing I am feeling? Is this feeling rooted in my current situation or from a past situation?

Here's an example using these five questions.

A person looks in the mirror and doesn't like the way their body looks. They feel unhappy with what they see and begin to spiral into self-loathing. This person then feels guilty for self-loathing, so they begin to self-loathe even more. To stop the spiral, practicing neutral self-honesty would be beneficial in this situation.

How can I validate these emotions I'm having? I feel unhappy with the way I look. This is okay. I am human and this is my humanity showing. I'm allowed to not always love how I look. This is not something I should be ashamed of.

Are these self-deprecating thoughts coming from a place of fairness? Well, I am comparing myself to other people's bodies, which isn't fair. I'm not them. I am me. I don't have to look like them. I am happy with the inner and outer beauty I currently possess. Bodies that look like this are normal and okay.

How will I dissolve this unhappiness with my body? I will do my best to be happy with my current state because I know my worthiness of love doesn't come from my appearance. Building on that, if this person does want to see some change in their physical appearance, they will take action by saying "I will set reasonable goals, research, set deadlines, and take action." I will follow through with these goals to build trust in myself. I will do it out of self-love because I want to have more energy and feel more confident. Wanting to feel more confident is okay. But I will NOT start changing my body unless it is out of self-love rather than self-loathing, because I am just as worthy and beautiful in my current state as well.

How will I do this out of self-love? I will acknowledge the root of this problem. My body discomfort derives from what I see in the media. These images are unrealistic and unfair to compare myself to. Measuring up to beauty standards will not make me happy. I will find happiness by reminding myself I am strong and capable. I am happy with who I am as a person within, that's what matters.

A big help for learning self-honesty is counseling and talking to people that you know have your best interest. As I've talked through situations like this, I've learned how exactly to process information in fairness by first doing it with someone else. When you are talking with someone else, it's like putting up bumpers when you go bowling. It allows for someone else to aid you in staying within the bumpers of fairness, stay away from the gutter of self-hatred or over analyzing, and move forward on your journey, rather than spiral into extended periods of anxiety, sadness, and stress.

Once you get better at neutral self-honesty you can start

getting more strikes without bumpers because your aim has been improved, you know how to guide yourself through tough situations with grace & compassion. You also learn when bumpers might be necessary because the ball or situation feels a little too heavy this time around, so it might get a little wobbly and head to the gutter. This time you can recognize that you do need bumpers. Because sometimes we need someone else to keep us from the gutter because this life is not meant to be walked alone. As independent as I'd like to be, I can't always rely on myself. That is okay. That is human.

Self-honesty builds foundations for future and current relationships:

Lastly, if we develop the skills of self-honesty, we build the foundation for future and current relationships. Because self-honesty brings peace within us and resolves inner turmoil, it allows our relationships and communication skills to improve. It allows us to be honest when we mess up. It also allows us to approach situations with a level head and trust in ourselves that we know how to sort out and validate emotion reasonably. If we do not learn to understand and process our inner turmoil, we will not have healthy relationships. Especially intimate relationships. I once heard Susan Piver, writer and meditation teacher, say in an interview that when you start a relationship you are separate, and as that gap closes, you will start reflecting your own inner turmoil on your partner because that gap has shrunk.

We tend to reflect our own insecurity and deep-rooted issues on others. If we can start working through those now, while we're young, we will be more at peace, have better communication skills, and have healthier, long-lasting relationships with friends, family, and a significant other.

## Why Do I Care So Much About Honesty?

We've talked about honesty with ourselves and with others. That brings us to the final dimension of honesty, which is most talked about: lying. Lying to get what you want or avoid a situation you don't want. Selfishness. Cheating, stealing, deceiving, and avoiding accountability.

Honesty is definitely the value I hold dearest to me. My mom instilled honesty in me from a young age. That was probably one of the strongest values taught in our home growing up.

First, she taught us to be honest with her. To trust in her with our emotions and feelings. She did this by exuding love and showing she believed in us. She is the type of person that exudes motherly love and radiates warmth. She taught me that it was safe for me to tell her when I messed up. I never felt I had to lie to my mom because I knew she would listen, if there was a consequence it would be reasonable and probably deserved. She guided with Christlike fairness and love. She taught me that the only way to build trust with someone was to be honest even when it's hard to be. I never had to hide anything from my mom growing up, because I trusted she would understand. She always saw my heart and intentions, even when I told her I screwed up. If I failed a test, I told her. If I got pulled over, I told her. If my friends were sneaking out and I wanted to go, I told her. I think trust is much more powerful than rules.

My mom allowed me to learn that once you share honesty with someone, you build accountability to the other person. You value trust over anything. Therefore, you don't lie. Ever. Because if you do that trust foundation gets shaky. It's easier to tell the hard truth than try and rebuild trust. Trust me.

Along with not lying, my mom instilled self-honesty in me. She taught me from a young age how to self-reflect. If I got into arguments with friends as a kid, she'd ask me "Where could you have done better to avoid the conflict?" She taught me starting in elementary school to validate my feelings, but also take accountability for my own addition to the argument. She taught me to recognize my downfalls. Being quick to self-honesty also allows us to quickly forgive, apologize, and mend relationships. I knew how to self-reflect because I grew up articulating my emotions to my mom in an open space, so I could later learn to articulate them to myself and process them in fairness.

Honesty with others and yourself takes time to develop. That is okay. You've got time, but start taking action. Make it a priority in your life to self-reflect and be honest with others and yourself. This will bring you peace.

I love you, and I'm proud of you. You have so much power inside you.

# 13

# Bread

In this chapter, we're talking about money. I want to note something in full transparency before we dive in and recognize that I am a white woman who comes from a middle to high income family. I recognize I have privileges others don't, but I wanted to bring up this topic because our money mindset is important and in this time of our life, money is an integral tool for survival and well-being. In that regard, I included this chapter hoping to share what I've learned from successful minds and personal study as it might help someone else flourish financially.

Your relationship with money matters. Money is not all we should care about in life, but it is a part of life. It is a tool that can free up our time, ease our anxieties, and give us an opportunity to make a more positive impact in the world. It's vital that we learn about it and improve our financial literacy. School doesn't usually teach this stuff, so at some point we must start learning about money ourselves. I'd recommend you learn sooner, rather than later. I'll be focusing specifically on money mindset or improving your relationship, understanding, and beliefs surrounding money. I want to note that money is a topic that has so many factors and variables as you move from situation to situation. Here, I am speaking from my experience, not on behalf of everyone's experience.

After finishing my first year of college, I headed back home for the summer and found myself looking for a new job. I hopped on Indeed and started looking through the job posts. I read through qualification section after qualification section, and almost every single one screamed that I wasn't qualified enough. I felt frustrated; although I didn't have the formal training they wanted, I had spent many, many hours learning a lot of these skills on YouTube and Google. I also knew I was an extremely fast learner who was always willing to get scrappy and figure out solutions. Regardless, I remember feeling discouraged and bummed out that I was probably going to have to settle for another job that I didn't really want that barely paid anything close to what I knew I was worth.

That was it! I knew what I was worth, why the frick was I letting these qualification sections beat me up?! Right then I decided I would refuse to settle. I wanted three things: to not work any sort of robotic sales or customer service job, work for a startup, and get paid better than my past jobs. I decided to pursue a marketing job, even though I had no experience at all, besides what I'd learned online, and what I practiced via my own social media. All that aside, I compiled a list of many marketing jobs I wanted to apply for, sent out my resume and cover letters, AND . . . *all* of them said no. I continued to search.

I finally stumbled across one job post for a marketing associate, someone who specialized in podcast production. I had started my own podcast two months prior, so I applied even though I didn't quite fit the rest of the qualifications.

It was a startup based out of Silicon Valley looking for someone to work remotely. I landed an interview, and the following week was offered the job. All I needed was one yes. I'd got everything I wanted: no robotic sales calls, the highest pay I'd ever received, working for a startup, and getting to do marketing. I got exactly what I wanted because I decided I could have it. Since then, I've come to learn and recognize my professional worth and have begun to do much less settling on a professional level.

When it comes to employment, know your worth. I find that often in our teens and early twenties we tend to settle for these Starbucks-esque jobs because we feel that's all the Universe has to offer us. That's simply not true. I'm not trying to shit on working at Starbucks – there are definitely situations where people don't have the energy, resources, privilege, certain educational resources, or time to have a "dream job" or a job that is totally ideal. I recognize that.

What I'm trying to say is, if you feel you have a great skill(s), want to learn skills that will advance your career in the future, or are worth more than what you currently get paid, don't hesitate to ask for more out of life. If we never even ask, the answer will always be no.

Not only that, but how much you get paid at a certain job is not always the best metric on deciding if you should take it. Say you have a choice between:

1. A retail job that pays well but has nothing to do with what you want to do with your career.
2. A job that pays just enough to make ends meet but is in the exact field and skill developer for your career path.

If it's possible for you on a financial and resource-based level, job number two might be the better choice. Why? Because it will connect you with people who will move you forward in your career. Making money and building a career is all about who you know. That sentiment has become very, *very* apparent as I've journeyed through this entrepreneurial lifestyle.

Second, if the low-paying job is teaching you a good skill that will help you for the rest of your career, that's HUGE. Think of it this way: "Money spends once, skills monetize *forever*." If you want to make more money, learning new skills can be an amazing way to do that. That's how I got that marketing job. I took a simple, cheap class on how to start a podcast, did some Google searching, got started, and landed a job two months later. Skills are king when it comes to making money. Online courses and Google searching have changed my life. Not only that, but skills are also *incredible* safety nets. When I dropped out of college and started my business, I didn't feel scared because I knew I had developed a set of skills that I could always monetize. No matter what happened, I knew I had backup. If I got scrappy enough, any of the skills I'd learned via courses and research could be monetized. That's a good feeling. It creates a lot less anxiety about money.

I've also found that if you're going to ask or want to receive more from life monetarily, you must be willing to give. People who are only takers and never givers suck. We don't want to be those people. From speaking with extremely wealthy individuals from a wide variety of backgrounds in person and on my podcast, I've found that the seemingly happiest and fulfilled people are the ones always ready and willing to give. If you want to make money, you must be willing to give it. Money works very similarly to Karma. What goes around comes around, good and bad. If you're willing to help others through the tool of money, more money will circle back to you. I can't explain exactly why this is, but it works! I think it's because the tighter we hold to something the more finite it becomes. We enter a scarcity mindset.

Let's say you only have one friend, but you've always wanted more close friends. If you often say to yourself, "I'll never make more friends," you'll probably never make more friends. The Universe is abundant with people, why are you blocking out possibilities? If you constantly tell yourself, "I'm broke, I'm broke, I'm broke," you'll never spend money. You never invest in others or yourself. You never do good deeds with your time and money. I'd be surprised if you ever become anything other than broke.

What you say and what you think matters, just like I've expressed in previous chapters. It is *crazy* how your thoughts impact your life, your bank account included.

As you start building your bank account, be careful about letting monetary success twist your mindset. I watched people start feeling genuinely, happier as they make more money. They think to themselves, "Well, I feel happier. It must be the things. It must be the money and the awards and the accolades." It isn't. It's important to remember that as we gain success, we might start feeling happier because of hard work and self-discipline, not because of the money. In order to achieve that success, you had to start disciplining yourself and acting in your own self-interest. You had to get control of your life and your mind.

**"Self-discipline is the definition of self-love."**
**— Will Smith**

When someone starts becoming more successful, it's often because they had to make massive changes in their life. They started practicing self-discipline, which grew their self-love. That's where that newfound happiness comes from. An increase in acting out of your own best interest or self-love. Success doesn't bring long-term joy because of the new life you've created for yourself, but because you've improved how you treat yourself. And an increase in self-love matters more than any type of monetary growth.

To wrap up, I want to put one specific debate to rest: 9–5 vs. entrepreneurs. In recent years, I've seen a lot of 9–5 workers hate on entrepreneurs for being "self-absorbed or slaves to capitalism", and I see entrepreneurs belittling 9–5 workers because they are "just making other people richer when they could make themselves richer instead." Here's the deal. Of course, I love entrepreneurship. It's how my brain has worked since I was a kid. I've had a business idea notebook since I was five. If you ever saw the movie *Robots* growing up, Bigweld's quote, "See a need, fill a need," was the most inspiring thing ever to my eleven-year-old brain. But how one person makes their income is not better than how someone else does. Not everyone's brain works the same. Not everyone has the same priorities. Not everyone has the same set of cards dealt to them in life.

I teach living in alignment. If you have the gift to choose what you do for work and how you do it in some capacity, do it in alignment with what feels best for you. If starting your own business around something you're passionate about feels right to you, do it. If you want to work a 9–5 that will get you home to your future family every day by dinner time, do it. If you like the idea of being in charge of your own schedule and becoming responsible for your own income via a business you started, do it. If you want to work for a large company and you just like your job okay, but it makes you good money that you can use to feed your passionate side projects, do it. If a job provides security and great benefits and that is the priority for you, do it. If you choose a career that doesn't pay much, but it brings you mass amounts of joy, please do it.

How one person lives in alignment is not better than how someone else lives in alignment. If how you live your life feels right to you, don't let anyone make you feel less than for that. The world needs all types of careers and people to keep it running. Do what is best for you, not what someone else says is best for you.

P.S. *Please* don't get a certain college degree just because your parents want you to get it. If you hate it, do not do it. It will only lead to resentment for your parents and feelings of unfulfillment in your life.

# 14

# Love, Marriage, Relationships, & What Not

Love, specifically romantic love . . . *deep breath.* Oh brother. Strap in for this chapter. It took me a while to even figure out where I wanted to start on this topic. I'll start by letting you into my journey with sir Cupid. Why? Because I think it's important to have these conversations as early as possible, as opposed to getting into long-term relationships or a marriage before actually establishing our beliefs and understanding of love. On top of that, I think you might see some of yourself in what I share, and I believe in the power of telling one's story. (Side note: when I say "love" in this chapter, I mean romantic love, though of course there are other very important forms of love.)

Love and I had a rough history, between my parents' struggling marriage and my feelings of being undesirable to guys growing up due to my height, some more masculine tendencies, and my lack of a super girly or flirty personality. My parents' marriage, especially, did a number on me (more so than I thought it would), and probably 45 percent or more of the people reading this have had a similar experience with their parents' relationship. On that note, I want to emphasize that, even though so many of us have developed trauma or triggers from our parents' marriages, it doesn't mean it hurts any less just because it might be a common pain. Just because divorce and poor marriages are so common doesn't invalidate the pain you feel and / or felt. It hurts, and it sucks. I'll touch on this more in a moment.

This suckish pain I felt around men, love, and marriage ran very deeply for me, but as mentioned in my healing portion of this book (chapter nine), suffering is a choice. I decided I wanted to heal, so I got to work. I went very, very deep into books, podcasts, therapy sessions, and articles around the topics of love during my healing process for about two years. And that shit *hurted*. Let me boil down what I've learned from that healing journey, examples of good and bad relationships in my life, and my experience with all types of love.

The three questions I dug very, very deep into myself and in research to answer:

1. What is love?
2. Why do we want love?
3. How do we make a long-term romantic relationship healthy?

## What Is Love?

To answer this question very simply, I'll start with the dictionary definition: "a feeling of strong or constant affection for a person." I think the keyword there is *constant*. Real love for someone is something that never goes away; it's constant. Real love is relatively unbreakable and that is why it is the most powerful force we as humans contain. We can dislike someone for a moment while simultaneously loving them. We can fall out of like with someone, but love is something, like I said, that I don't think really goes away. You might not be in love with who someone has become, but I think a piece of that love for who someone used to be will always reside in us. Love's constant nature is also what makes it so scary. Once we give it away and surrender to it, it's very, very hard to break that kind of bond. Along with love being a constant, powerful force, it is also not just a feeling or emotion.

Love is a skill. Love is something we have to intentionally learn how to do, if we want to do it well. Love is something we have to work at. Love has to be nurtured and watered and cared for.

Love is also sacrifice and compromise. I heard a quote that describes this perfectly:

**"Love one another but make not a bond of love. Let it rather be a moving sea between the shores of your souls."**
**— Kahlil Gibran**

That is love. Love is an exchange of energy that is in a constant ebb and flow. It never flows at one specific intensity or capacity. It rushes between two people, finding a balance between chaos and harmony. This is why I think the saying "relationships are 50/50" is totally untrue. A desire to perform in love at a constant 50/50 with a partner is unrealistic thinking. Love is showing up at 70 when your partner is only at a 30. Love is communicating when you're at a 40 and you need your partner to pick up the extra 10 that day. Love is compromise and sacrifice, which is why it is such a good teacher.

In conclusion, to me, love is a powerful force, a skill, and a teacher.

## Why Do We Want Love?

**"No matter what we do, love saturates our lives in every possible way. Even when we try to escape it, it finds us - if merely to tease us with what we could have"**
**— Alain de Botton**

WHY THE HELL DO WE WANT LOVE?! I racked my brain for years on this one. It's painful and devastating and scary and so, so, so much work. And yet, it's the most desired thing on this planet. This makes *no sense* considering our brains are wired to take the path of least resistance and love is *not* that. So, what's the deal? Here's what I figured out and I hope it will bring some peace to those of you that need it.

My coldness toward the idea of love solidified around sixteen or seventeen, when many things about my parents' marriage began to present themselves. To explain my "coldness" here is an example: I'd go to a wedding and feel devastated for the bride. She just wrecked her entire life, I thought. I felt like we were all there celebrating a tragedy. Absolutely no happy feelings on Livi's end.

Despite those feelings, and it might shock some people to know (my family might not even know this now) – I've always been a romantic. I've watched a good majority of the romance movies on Netflix, I like cheesy gestures, and I like when people are happy together. Regardless of some of our hard exteriors, I think we're all a bit like this. Funny how we as humans can be a paradox like that. But boy, did I suppress those cheesy feelings in my late teens.

If you've ever read or seen *Little Women*, Jo is basically me in a fictional character. Loving, intense, peacemaker, writer, sister, daughter, loyal to a fault, honest, stubborn, a dreamer, conflicted . . . I'm probably a bit more relaxed and it takes quite a bit to get me angry, but overall, we're very similar. I was in the midst of my love-healing journey when I first watched that movie. Near the end, Jo says, "Women have minds and souls as well as just hearts, and they've got ambition and talent as well as just beauty. And I'm sick of people saying that love is all a woman is fit for. I'm so sick of it! But – I'm so lonely!" I sobbed like a baby in my theater seat. Never had my feelings been articulated so perfectly.

Growing up, all I heard were love songs, and all girls seemed to talk about was anything related to the love genre. I got sick of having to tell a group of people I'd never kissed anyone (had my first kiss at sixteen with some random dude to get it over with) and having to feel shame about it. I got sick of being told I was supposed to desire marriage when pretty much all I saw were bad examples of it. I got sick of hearing girls say they'd just marry rich rather than believing in their own ability to provide for themselves. I got sick of society making me feel like I needed to fit the male gaze that I felt so far from (and I didn't at all mind being far from it.) I got sick of many of the women around me getting more excited about a woman getting married than getting a big job promotion, getting into a college or graduate program, or starting a business. I got sick of the first question asked at family gatherings being if I was dating anyone. I got sick of the games and the guessing and the peer obsession. I felt like the world was trying to reduce me to my relationship status, and I got *so very* sick of it.

So, I started to hate it. Well, strongly dislike – hate is a strong word, as my mom always says. I started to convince myself I hated it from a young age, so truly my issue with love started there, before the crumbling of my view of it from my parents' marriage. In the midst of my love-hating, in all honesty, I desired it painfully deep in my loneliest moments, which enraged me even further. I was independent from a very young age and never understood my desire for another person. I grew up with two parents who rarely asked for help; they were scrappy, and we were all fighters. That was the mindset. If I loved myself enough, shouldn't I be good enough for myself, I thought?

Here is a small section of something I wrote amidst my healing journey:

"Shouldn't we be content with our thoughts and produce enough self-love to not let loneliness overpower us. I just find myself frustrated that our spiritual design isn't enough for itself. If we were made in an All-Powerful being's image shouldn't we be enough for ourselves, gaps not needed to be filled by others? Sometimes love feels like weakness. Craving genuine, intimate love feels like weakness. I want to be enough for myself, but apparently, God did not design me for that. Frustrating. Is God enough for himself? Is there an eternal power in the connection of two that doesn't lie within an individual? The only reason I can find is God gave me a desire to love to humble my desire for control. To learn and grow."

Truly, at the time, I felt like an inability to be on your own, to not be 100 percent independent, was a weakness. By the way, if you feel like this, hyper independence is also a trauma response, so that might be something to look into for you.

Now here is how I found my peace and understanding of why we desire love so strongly. How I melted my coldness, per se. These answers I found for myself are heavily based on God and spirituality, and I don't expect you to agree with them and I'm not delivering them to you as fact. I believe spirituality is very fluid and, as far as that goes, people should do what works for them and brings them joy and peace. That being said, I want to share these three things in case someone needs to hear them.

## 1. Our desire for love is innate

I have come to the conclusion that a desire to love and be loved is innately built into us as humans. We have a deep, spiritual desire to be linked to another person. In the spirit of complete transparency, I can't quite explain this. Regardless, through meditation and prayer, that's what I've discovered. It goes deeper than just a chemical reaction in our brain, I think it's also a very spiritual desire. Let me offer you two quotes:

**"Love is our connection to an immortal, spiritual realm that reaches beyond our own short lives."**
**— Alain De Botton**

**"We are all thousand-watt souls with 40-watt bulbs."**
**— Harvard Negotiation Project**

These two quotes also help articulate my belief that we have a very spiritually rooted desire to be linked because something about love allows us to access more of our souls and power, that I don't believe we can access on our own. Love allows us to access a higher frequency or "wattage" that our souls contain. If you look at a frequencies of consciousness scale it shows you the vibrational frequencies (energy) different emotions create, and love is one of the highest frequencies on that scale. So, as someone that believes in a Creator and has a relationship with that Creator, I respect and have faith in the construction of how my spirit, energy, and body were created. In that, I found my first bit of peace. Deciding to just surrender through faith in my spiritual design.

## 2. God is Love

God, an almighty and all-knowing being chooses to love his children (us) and open himself to vulnerability. I believe in a very loving God. That is why he cries for us when we are struggling because loving deeply also comes with pain. He doesn't need to choose this, but he does. God chooses to love. God is the greatest teacher, and He is Love, so Love is the greatest teacher. That is why we must experience love, to learn. (I'd also like to mention I use the term "He" lightly here. I believe and have a relationship with a Heavenly Mother or Divine Feminine Energy as well, so I use universe, God, energy all very interchangeably and fluidly.  I also believe in connecting with the energy of the universe and how we interact with it. My beliefs, and how I look at higher power is a bit fluid, so that's a whole other topic we need not get into here.)

## 3. Choose your suffering

Finally, as I mentioned earlier in this book, most decisions we make result in negative and positive experiences no matter what we choose. All choices come with forms of suffering or pain no matter what they are. This applies to love. We must choose our form of suffering. If we choose to be single, or not intentionally explore love, we experience the pains of loneliness and what could have been. If we choose to fight for love, with another person, we experience the pains of contention, compromise, and sacrifice. With that logic, I thought to myself, well which suffering do I prefer? There isn't a right or wrong answer, but for me, I decided on option two. I'd prefer to experience new suffering and learn through experiences with another person I'm deeply connected with. I'd also like to enjoy the positive and new experiences of option two with someone else. Walking myself through those two options gave me my final bit of peace.

Why do we want love? Those are the answers I have for you right now. If none of those do it for you, then I'll leave you with this answer . . . we just do. I've found that sometimes accepting that some things just are, can also bring us peace.

## How Do We Make A Long-Term Romantic Relationship Healthy?

**"We seem to know far too much about how love starts &
recklessly little about how it might continue."
— Alain De Botton**

That's the question. How does one make love continue in a joyful and healthy manner? Truly the answer to this question is very situational, which is why I'm a big advocate for couples and sex therapy. There doesn't have to be something wrong with your relationship to consider going to therapy. Therapy is simply a tool that can make your connection even stronger. Everyone and each relationship is different. Having said that, here are some mindset shifts and concepts that can benefit any relationship in the long term. Most of these can also apply to friendships and family relationships as well.

### 1. Honesty is one of the keys to relationship sustainability.

Since I grew up with a terminally ill parent for six years, whenever the topic of family came up on dates, it wasn't the most fun conversation for me. I started to really dislike the typical "yeesh, haven't heard that one yet" face that people made when I told them, especially after my dad died. I don't mind at all talking about my family's experience with my dad's illness and passing, but understandably, it tends to throw people off guard when I'm on a date. If you aren't used to talking about death, it makes you uncomfortable. I get it.

One specific instance: I went on a date with a guy I met in college. I figured on this particular date I'd try to avoid this six-year period of my life altogether. I decided to act like we were still a solid, and very much alive, family of four. When he asked what my dad did for work, I said he was a pharmacist. When I talked about my dad, I used present tense. Instead of "He spoke Spanish," I said, "He speaks Spanish." Very bad idea. Why I did this, not sure. Near the end of the night he was driving me back to my car and we were talking about a vacation my mom, sister, and I had been on. He suddenly asked, "where was your dad when you guys went?" My brain left my body. Unable to come up with a lie fast enough I panicked and said, "He died." (Don't worry, you can laugh.) That boy looked so very confused. I didn't even explain myself. I just got in my car and left.

What did we learn from this, folks? Don't ever try to start a relationship or first date with a lie. Don't lie about who you are, where you come from, what you do, how much money you make, what you believe in. Nothing good will come out of it. You will not build anything healthy and sustainable off lies. While in a relationship, don't lie about how you feel or what's going on in your life. Nothing good will come from it. Lies turn into more lies. Honesty. Honesty. Honesty.

**2. If you don't heal, it will present itself in your relationship.**
When you first start dating someone, you see yourself as a very separate person from your partner. Think of one bead of red paint (you) and one bead of blue paint (your partner) on a paint palette. At this point in a relationship, the start, it's much easier to see our unhealed trauma and internal conflicts as something very separate from our partner, because the paint hasn't started to mix.

But as time passes and your lives and habits begin to mix, that separation of what is an issue from your past and what is an issue within your relationship becomes blurred. The issues that we knew were ours because they were bright red, start to mix with our relationship and partner (the blue) and slowly it all turns purple. We lose track of what is a trigger from our past that we are projecting onto a partner and what is something that is actually to be worked through within the relationship. Soon we start to irrationally blame our partner for our internal conflicts because we feel that they are triggering them, when truly we just haven't healed from our past.

For example, say you grew up in a household where the main form of communication during conflict tended to be yelling, because of this you lose your temper easily because that is what was always modeled at home. You never work on changing this trigger that you developed as a kid. Later in life, you enter a relationship, and all seems well. As you and your partner's lives begin to mix, the relationship gets more serious, and you become much more comfortable with sharing your crazy, irrational sides around one another. Suddenly, your relationship seems to be sliding downhill because you find yourself yelling at your partner often. You blame your partner for making you yell all the time, which creates a lot of resentment and tension. That's called projection. The issue here isn't that your partner is "making" you do anything. The issue is from your unhealed past, not necessarily within the quality of your relationship. That is past trauma or unattended issues bubbling up. If you want a healthy relationship in the future, or right now, start healing asap.

### 3. Maintenance is everything.

Healthy relationships require *constant* maintenance. A small conflict or miscommunication is almost never too small that it shouldn't be talked about or addressed, at least briefly. Small issues build up if they aren't addressed and can result in a lot of resentment, which causes even bigger problems. Like I said, love is a skill, if you want to be good at it, it takes work. If something bothered you, don't brush it under the rug. If you have a keeper, they'll also be happy that you mentioned this bothersome moment to them because they don't want you to feel resentment either.

### 4. The only thing you can control in a relationship is you.

The key to finding someone that you can build a healthy, long-lasting relationship with is asking yourself: does this person have flaws that I can happily accept and not feel resentful over? Not only asking yourself, what do I want in a significant other, but what flaws would I be able to work with? Also, what type of person could work well with my flaws? For example, you have a great relationship with someone who is late to everything, but you are ten minutes early to a default. Is that something you could accept about the other person and choose to not get upset over? If you have a hard time with not feeling jealousy towards others, what type of person could accept that trait in you? Of course, we can grow, and our partner can grow and improve as a person, but we will always be imperfect. So, I'd take your flaws and your S/O flaws at face value, instead of expecting someone to change.

You cannot assume your partner will change. You either accept them with their flaws and have compassion for their limitations or move on. Those are the two options. I had a conversation with a couple's therapist, Shane Hirkel, on my podcast, *Today is the Future*. Below I added a snippet that illustrates this concept really well.

Shane: "How do I express my own boundaries for myself while respecting your boundaries? Or respecting who you are? How do I move into compassion? For example, if I've expressed to my wife that I'm afraid of dogs. We go on a walk one day, a dog walks down the sidewalk, and I move to the other side of the road. My wife doesn't come with me. I might then move into the victim's stance. 'Woe is me; my wife doesn't support me and doesn't understand me.' The victim stance is where 99 percent of violence in the world comes from. Every perpetrator believes they are the victim in their own story and also believes they are the hero in their own story.

So, because I'm filled with contempt for my wife, because she didn't run across the street with me, I feel entitled in the way that I talk to her. 'Why didn't you come across the street with me, that was so lame?!' Which is terrible, which is blame-y, which is harsh, which is critical, which are all things that are terrible for relationships. I'm attacking from the victim position . . .

What we have to do is take responsibility for ourselves. This is where people get it very messed up. Most of the time we're in the victim stance and we're waiting for our partner to do something different in order for us to feel okay. This is codependence. I'm living my life as a miserable victim waiting for others to change. This is the definition of being disempowered. It's an awful way to live. The goal is not to change my wife. The goal is for me to move into self-empowerment and move into compassion for her limitations. We must realize that we have it within ourselves to see the world in a way that makes us feel empowered."

We will never be perfect humans, and neither will our partner. Either find self-empowerment in what you have, or it might not be a good fit.

## 5. Stop trying to be right.

In disagreements, we try so hard to be right. We let our ego take over and refuse to live with someone not having our same opinion, which is usually extremely correct. When it comes to relationships this mindset is *very* destructive. The goal is not to determine who is right but do our best to accept both stories. How can we do this? Recognizing that neither story is right, there are just two different perceptions. We perceive interactions differently based on the information we have, or don't have, and our differences in our mental wiring. Make your default putting yourself in your partner's shoes. Empathy is an amazing tool to remove added resentment and anger from a relationship.

Let's say you go to the grocery store with your S/O. You generally like to take your time grocery shopping. As you proceed to squish the sides of a dozen avocados to find the perfect one, your partner goes wandering off leaving you to shop alone. You don't like this because you wanted to spend time with them while you shopped. As you finish up with the fruits and veggies section of the store your partner comes hustling back with the rest of the grocery list. You feel very irritated and upset. It would be easy here to give the silent treatment or get upset, but let's look at each perception.

Perception #1 (you): You grew up grocery shopping with a parent who always took their time in the store, so that's how you shop. You wanted to go grocery shopping with your S/O today because you weren't able to spend much time together this week. The fact that they left you made you feel like they didn't want to spend time with you and wanted to get the grocery trip over with. You feel sad and unwanted.

Perception #2 (your partner): They don't like being in the grocery store and prefer to get it off the to-do list. They thought that it would be helpful and generous of them to finish off the list, so you both could head home and watch a movie together. When they came back and you were upset, it made them feel confused and bothered.

Neither perception is right, just two different stories. We often automatically assume ill intent when we are upset. If we can take a step back and look at a situation for what it really is, it's much easier to stay calm and rational when working through conflict.

Taking a step back doesn't look like you saying what they did was wrong: "Why did you leave me, that was so rude."

It's starting with how you feel: "I wanted to spend time with you while we shopped so when you left it made me sad."

Starting with your perception, and not assuming theirs, is a much healthier plan of action. That being said, recognizing their perception doesn't make your emotions invalid, it just gives you a greater capacity to validate theirs. The outcome of the situation I mentioned could be anger and spending no time together at all for the rest of the day OR you each explain your perception, apologize for the confusion and lack of communication and move forward with your day. I'd prefer to move forward with my day and not expend energy on such a small interaction.

**6. We often look for familiarity more than what's healthy.**
Say you grew up in a family that rarely expressed their emotions to one another. You generally find yourself dating people that are a bit closed off and not very emotionally available, like yourself. At some point, you start dating someone that is very open about their emotions. Their emotional availability makes you really uncomfortable. On the flip side, in this relationship, you don't find yourself constantly chasing words of affirmation or questioning what's in the other person's head. You feel at ease. This makes you feel like maybe you aren't into this person as much as people you've dated in the past because your emotions seem to be much more stable. You break up with them because it feels so unfamiliar, and you continue on with your string of emotionally unavailable partners.

This is a type of self-sabotage. Oftentimes in relationships we look for familiar and not necessarily healthy. If your parents yell a lot, you tend to feel more familiar and comfortable in a relationship where you yell at each other often. If your ex was codependent, you might find a healthy, self-empowered relationship super uncomfortable.

As you enter new relationships ask yourself, is this uncomfortable or unfamiliar just because I've never experienced healthy before? Am I mistaking being at peace with boredom? Am I mistaking emotional stability as having less interest?

### 7. No one will ever check all the boxes for you.
A short story I wrote about always waiting for the perfect person:

*She had a worn, folded paper in hand with a long column of checkboxes. I thought it quite possible that it was a grocery or errands list of sorts. She had wrinkles that creased her eyelids and forehead that seemed induced by stress and longing. She wore a long purple dress with a gleaming broach clipped neatly to her chest. She sat adjacent to a man in a small pink coffee shop. The man was of similar age and was enthusiastically telling a story. His radiant smile shining with each word. He reminded me of the lovely, old man next door to my childhood home that treated me like a granddaughter. Telling me beautiful stories of the world and handing me pearly, white tulips from his little garden. As the man told his invigorating story the woman barely looked up. She was looking at the folded paper. Every so often she would lift a pen to the paper and check a box. As kind as the man across from the table seemed to be, she barely paid him any mind. She stayed fixated on the paper. After some time had passed, the sunlight hit her folded paper just right. The paper was now transparent in my vision, I noticed all the boxes were checked but one. Quite suddenly, and to the man's surprise, she crumpled the paper with its last checkbox still empty, slipped it into her handbag, rose from her seat, and walked briskly out the door. The man looked blindsided. I watched as the woman trudged, unenthusiastically towards the small, blue coffee shop further down the street.*

If we are so fixated on a checklist of traits or what a person must be, we'll probably always be looking. We will continue, coffee shop date after coffee shop date, into our old age. No one will be everything for you and you can't expect to be everything for someone else. That's why it's important to have hobbies and friends outside of a serious relationship, to check those extra boxes. You can't expect a partner to check every single box for you. Perfect relationships don't exist because perfect people don't exist. Stop looking for perfect. Love's beauty is partially rooted in its imperfections.

### 8. Prepare now, rather than later.
Even if you aren't in a relationship right now, or plan on getting married anytime soon, prepare now. If you can learn about communication, love, marriage, empathy, red flags, and how to make a relationship work now, you'll have a much smoother time later. Study before the test.

Not only this but work on yourself. We attract people like ourselves. Heal, work on your personal fulfillment, work on your mindfulness and emotional intelligence, and work on valuing yourself. Become the person you want to attract.

**"The arrow doesn't seek the target, the target seeks the arrow, our souls are infinitely magnetic."**
**— Matthew McConaughey**

# 15

# A Self-Confidence Root Canal Won't Cut it

**W**hen the dentist is mentioned, you might initially remember the anxiety or dread you get on your way to that six-month check-up appointment. If you're weird like me, you might get a little bit of excitement for the feeling of leaving the office with freshly, smooth, and cleaned teeth. Let me explain to you the concept of biological dentistry, a.k.a. holistic dentistry, and the emphasis these dentists put on the treatment of the whole person and overall health, rather than just the symptoms of dental disease.

Disclaimer:

1. I'm not teaching you about root canals for the sake of it. There is a reason behind me giving you all this (at first glance) unwarranted dental knowledge.
2. I'm not trying to promote holistic dentistry; I couldn't tell you if this stuff works –this is just an analogy to help you in your development process.

Alrighty, let's get into it.

The dentistry you and I are familiar with is traditional. You are told you should get a check-up every six months or so. They give your teeth a good power washing. The dentist comes in and sticks a tiny mirror in your mouth, writes some stuff down, and rinses and repeats this process.

Holistic dentists take a different approach. They generally don't fully support the modern medicine idea that we should have a different doctor check on each area of our body separately. You go to an optometrist for your eyes, podiatrist for your feet, gynecologists for vagina owners, so on and so forth. To them, it doesn't make much sense because it's all the same body. All one system working together; therefore, wouldn't it make more sense to look into how each part is affecting all the other parts? Holistic dentists explore how disease and infection in the mouth cause negative side effects throughout the body. It's similar to how many gastroenterologists talk about how your gut health severely affects the rest of the body and mental stability. German physician Dr. Reinhard Voll assesses that around 80 percent of all sickness is related to, at least partially, problems in your mouth.

Here's an example of how a traditional dentist versus a holistic dentist would approach a tooth infection.

Claudio has been experiencing a lot of pain in his tooth. He can't chew on that side, and it aches throughout the day. He goes to a dentist to get it checked out and is told that he is experiencing tooth decay because bacteria have entered the root of his tooth.

A traditional dentist might land on a root canal procedure for treatment. This is where a dentist goes in and removes the infected pulp that is inside the root of the tooth. In this scenario, Claudio leaves with the tooth intact, but there are chances that issues with that tooth could still arise, resulting in additional procedures.

A holistic dentist takes an alternate route. Because holistic dentists believe that your mouth can affect all areas of your body, they might prefer to remove Claudio's entire tooth. This is because although a root canal works to remove the decay within the tooth and then preserve the tooth's remains, the root of the tooth is still dead. Holistic dentists believe that leaving that dead tooth in the mouth can cause serious side effects throughout the body, ripple effects. Possible hearing issues, sinus infection, muscle tension, and more. That dead tooth is a bacteria hub, an infection center, and an accident waiting to happen.

Self-love and self-confidence work similarly to this example of Claudio's tooth mishap. Self-love and self-confidence are not the same things. You can have self-confidence and still have a deep lack of self-love. Self-confidence is defined as "a feeling of trust in one's abilities, qualities, and judgment," while self-love is defined as "regard for one's own well-being and happiness."

These two traits do not grow on the same tree. Self-confidence is much more a way of doing, and self-love falls under a way of being. Self-confidence is a matter of the brain, logic, and a tool for success in many areas. Self-love is a matter of the heart and will serve as a guide in living a happy life.

In relation to Claudio's tooth, when we exude self-confidence, we can appear very solid and happy on the outside, such as a tooth after a root canal. In all reality, the tooth is still dead, regardless of its shiny appearance, like our lack of self-love. True self-love is not about just appearing shiny and confident, but treating our dead roots and replacing that old, rotten tooth with a new one. Replacing our old ideas of who we are and what we deserve with new ideas that allow us to value ourselves. True self-love requires you to treat your internal conflicts at their source, which in turn will create a more authentic self-confidence that is rooted in self-love.

Let me introduce you to Leroy. Leroy is a resourceful and top-of-the-line businessman. All his life Leroy radiated charisma, and people naturally gravitated towards him. Because of this, in his late twenties, he found he had a natural talent for selling. I mean this guy could sell ice to a polar bear, a dildo to a nun. He was incredible, and everyone saw him as such.

By his early thirties, he had been working for the same company for about seven years. He sat, calling and typing and chatting and scheduling and emailing and selling and selling and selling, until he was suddenly interrupted by a colleague. His colleague, Gina, leaned over his computer and told him he needed to go grab a seat in the boss's office.

Each person on the sales floor had a quarterly meeting with Ted, their boss, about how they had been doing reaching quotas. Leroy plopped down in the dark mahogany chair and started counting the pencils Ted had neatly arranged in a row on his desk. Ted walked into the room smiling and reached out to Leroy for a firm, hefty handshake.

Ted reviewed Leroy's numbers and grinned. He told Leroy they looked fantastic as always and joked that Leroy could teach everybody else a thing or two. Leroy laughed and agreed with Ted. Their meeting ended, Leroy rose to his feet, headed for the door, and heard Ted passively say to himself,

"That boy is quite the swindler, impressive."

Leroy's stomach sank. "A swindler?" he thought.

With that one word, his whole worldview was flipped. He stared at the list of names to contact on his desk, and for the first time in seven years took a hard look at his life. He couldn't believe it. Shit, he *was* a swindler. He hated who he'd become. He had been so caught up in the money and his natural abilities that he rarely had a second thought about the daily, unethical business tactics he had slowly developed. The whole company sold with two faces, and Ted congratulated them for it.

At this moment Leroy is a perfect example of great self-confidence with a deep lack of self-love. He trusted in his "abilities, qualities, and judgment" as a salesman, but had come to completely lack regard for his "own well-being and happiness." Unfortunately, we all are at risk of becoming Leroys. If you feel you might already be a Leroy, it's never too late to reunite with your self-love. To clarify, there is nothing wrong with being self-confident. Many people use their self-confidence for good, for change, but we must be using both tools in unison. As we confidently use our most evolved abilities to succeed, we need to let our self-love guide us, humble us, and give ourselves compassion.

In all reality, the ways we lack self-love can manifest in ways we don't even realize. In subtle ways, that is not so unethical, noticeable, and Leroy-esque.

As I mentioned earlier my dad was diagnosed with Amyotrophic Lateral Sclerosis (ALS, also known as Lou Gehrig's) when I was eleven years old. I want to share with you my family situation growing up for three reasons.

1. Sharing your story allows people the capacity to share theirs
2. I'll reference it a few times throughout this book
3. It portrays a great example of lacking self-love and subtle ways that lack of love can surface itself

Here is a snippet of the book I started writing at sixteen about our family's experience with ALS that I ended up not finishing. I felt it wasn't the right book for me to finish. But for this book, I figured, why rewrite a story that's already been written? Cue the writings of the Livi who had just got her driver's license:

"After one year of visiting many doctors, receiving multiple diagnoses, many tests, and a couple of surgeries this was the day his symptoms concluded. He had been having severe breathing issues, cramping throughout the body, muscle fasciculations, weakness in his hands, and rapid weight loss.

The doctor came into the room and began to explain, after many tests, trials, and previous diagnoses, the doctors had concluded that my Dad had ALS.

ALS, often referred to as Lou Gehrig's Disease, is a progressive, fatal neuromuscular disease that slowly robs a person of their ability to walk, use their hands, speak, swallow and eventually breathe. ALS has no treatment or cure. ALS patients will inevitably become paralyzed. Your muscles degrade until all you are is skin and bones. You are in constant pain as well as the inability to take a deep breath, improper blood circulation, lack of energy, and inability to speak.

The doctors gave my dad 2–5 years to live and told him to get your affairs together, you are going to die.

It has been about 4 years since December 12th, 2012. My Dad has lost roughly 90% of the movement in his legs, 100% in his feet, 60% in his neck, and 80% in his arms. He has lost 65 lbs. and now has a feeding tube, tracheostomy, and ventilator, and is completely dependent on others for transport and daily needs. His lungs are only at 30% capacity and continue to lose strength. Not sure what 30% lung capacity feels like? Try going on a run only breathing through two coffee straws. He's been doing that for 4 years.

Life is hard but if we learn from others and ourselves, we can, as my Dad always says, 'Finish Strong.'"

Fast forward to today. I can tell you what happened next. My Dad eventually passed away on December 1, 2018, and that last year and a half he was living was quite the fight for the whole family. Along with my Dad, of course, my mom bore the brunt. That woman knows how to fight like hell while simultaneously being an angel sent from heaven.

Nobody realizes the back-breaking work a 24-hour caregiver has to go through. Anxiety, emergencies, overnight hospital stays, being stuck in the house, becoming distant from friends, body pain from lifting and adjusting my Dad (he was a big dude, 6'5"), a loss of self, dressing him, bathing him, learning all the functions of a CNA and respiratory therapist, depression, frustration, a loss of personal hobbies, low energy, sadness, dealing with lots of poop and pee (I mean, it got gruesome; smells I've never smelled before), the list could go on. Just getting him ready took about two hours with my sister and me helping, even him having a bowel movement often took one to five days. Everything took time.

This was all my mom did all day, every day for five years. She never did the bare minimum either, she always did her best to make my Dad comfortable and as healthy as possible. Nurses and doctors at the hospitals were amazed at my quadriplegic dad's condition with my Mom as his caregiver. One hospital even offered her a job, of course she didn't take it. She wasn't about to be a caregiver for longer than she needed to. We can all learn a lot from my mom's example – her patience, her love, her resilience, and her adaptability. However, my mom did have her downfalls, as we all do. We're all imperfect human beings.

Why did I tell you all this? Weren't we talking about self-love and self-confidence? Yes. Let me get back to that. As I said, my mom had her downfalls, one of them being she struggled with accepting help from others while my dad was sick. She grew up in a poor family, the youngest of eleven kids. She had learned to be scrappy and self-sufficient. My mom didn't receive much guidance or assistance growing up, so she developed a mindset of not needing anyone else to help. Throughout my dad's sickness, my mom had a really hard time letting people help us. Our neighbors were so kind. They'd bring us dinner, drive my sister and me to practices, shovel out snow, sit with my Dad, and help make his life a little more exciting, but after that my mom wasn't a big fan of anyone else helping. Cleaning, laundry, hanging up clothes, helping get my dad ready, and all the stuff that required more detail? She had a system and didn't want it interrupted. I believe, and so does she, that this stemmed from her childhood, but also her desire to control her life where she could as it was spinning out of control. Many people encouraged and were willing to help pay for (so kind, might I add), her to put my Dad in an assisted living facility, or hire an all-day nurse. My Mom didn't do it. The occasional hired help usually didn't do as good a job as my mom did, so self-sufficient Leah went about caregiving mainly on her own, with my sister and I's help for a few hours a day. She also didn't want my sister and me to help too much because she wanted our lives to stay as normal as possible, bless her soul.

Nearing the end of my Dad's life, my Mom started doing a lot of self-reflection. She finally came to a point where she started giving away control. She let people help us pack when we moved, let people organize rooms, let people do her laundry, and finally hired a college student to help her out with caregiving a few times a week. She was loosening the reins. This was because she had reached heightened levels of exhaustion, but also because, amidst all this self-reflection, she had started to love herself, she told me. She realized she had gone pretty much her whole life not loving herself or what she saw in the mirror. She had self-confidence in her abilities, but lacked self-love, and never regarded her own well-being or happiness, only everybody else's. She realized letting people help you when they ask is an act of love from both of you.

Years after my Dad's death my Mom has now reached a level of self-love that is incredible. She is unrecognizable compared to the state she was in while caring for my dad, and even compared to times prior. She has started to act, for one of the first times in her life, with her well-being and happiness as one of her top priorities.

Making your well-being a top priority isn't selfish; it's self-love. How you feel matters. Your happiness matters. Let people help you when you hit rock bottom. Act in accordance with self-love, with your happiness in mind. Self-love is also self-control. Writing this book has severely tested my self-love. When I feel anxious, uninterested, or scared to write, which is pretty much every day, I ask myself: Do you love yourself? Are you acting in accordance with your self-love? I reply to myself, "Of course I love myself," and so I push through the uncertainty and make my happiness a top priority. Productivity and creativity make me happy, so I get up and make my well-being the top priority.

My Mom not wanting to receive help is a lack of self-love, but also an act of self-sabotage. Self-sabotage is defined as "behaviors or thought patterns that hold you back and prevent you from doing what you want to do." Being satisfied that you tried and happy you didn't succeed. Pretending to care for your happiness, while subconsciously knowing that you aren't.

For example, knowing you have a great comment in class and raising your hand just as the teacher is no longer taking comments. Trying, but being happy you didn't succeed. Or, going on a date and telling yourself it will suck. Had you not had that mindset before, maybe you would have enjoyed yourself. But instead, you're satisfied that you tried and happy the date sucked, just as you said you knew it would.

Here is a list of a few more examples of self-sabotage:

1. You're scared to do things by yourself
2. You rarely go outside your comfort zone
3. You don't set healthy boundaries in your relationships
4. You're always comparing yourself to others
5. Always waiting for the "right" moment to start something

Don't feel bad if any of these describe you. It's perfectly human. If none of them do, it's still good to check yourself and see if you're self-sabotaging in any other ways.

Here's how you can check yourself:

*Step 1* is to increase your self-awareness. Write down on a piece of paper what usually stops you from achieving your goals or living most authentically to you. Focus on the actions you do that aren't in your best interest. Take responsibility.

*Step 2* is to practice recognizing these self-sabotaging actions immediately when you do them. Pay closer attention when you feel unfulfilled, unsatisfied, or empty.

*Step 3* is to have a plan of action when you catch yourself self-sabotaging or about to self-sabotage. A plan of action that can be deployed in most self-sabotaging moments is to ask yourself before you take action, "Will what I'm doing increase my love for myself?" If it won't, don't do it.

Here are a few more plan of action examples you might use:

If you catch yourself comparing yourself to others, have a self-reflection regime in place, such as meditation, journaling, and/or having someone you love and trust bring you back to reality (I talk about how to do all these things in this book.)

If you often wait to start working on your dreams or projects, do some research on perfectionism and how to dilute it.

If you rarely get outside your comfort zone, gradually do things that healthily get you outside of that box. The final resort? Do what a friend of mine does: tape a piece of paper to the back of your door that says NO SELF SABOTAGE.

Keep working on your self-confidence and self-love. This

isn't an overnight or linear progression. This is something we can always work on, that's what makes it so beautiful. You can constantly be shaping who you are.

# 16

# Build-A-Parent Workshop

As I mentioned in my introduction, this book has grown with me in a lot of ways. It was not only meant to help you grow as a person. It's a record of my growth as well. One major life change that occurred while I was writing this book was my solo move from Utah to San Diego.

Before I moved, the only close friend I had left in-state was my dearest homie, Rachel. As a goodbye present, I decided to take her on a surprise trip to Build-A-Bear Workshop. She'd never gone as a kid and felt like she needed the experience. Some of you may have experienced the good ole time of going to Build-A-Bear as a kid. If you haven't been there, it's a magical place where your choice of teddy bear skin is semi-aggressively filled with white stuffing and given to you in full custody with no proper screening. I loved it as a kid. (Side note: I had the plan to write this Build-A-Bear-inspired chapter a year before actually writing it, and in that year of time before writing it, I actually went on Build-A-Bear's podcast. I feel like that's a kind of cool and ironic detail to share . . . anyway.) Rachel and I took our day trip to Build-A-Bear, and our matching bears were born, Sheila and Neve.

Inspired by Build-A-Bear Workshop, I decided to make my own workshop for you within my book. Instead of transporting you to your past childhood memories and building a bear, my workshop is a catalyst to transport you into your ideal life and build a better mindset.

## Welcome to Build-A-Parent Workshop

Let me explain to you our philosophy here at Build-A-Parent Workshop.

No one had a say in which uterus they ended up in. We didn't get to choose who raised us, where we were raised, or how we were raised. Regardless if you feel like you got dealt a great hand or a crappy hand in the parent department, you can still choose who you are the child of.

I want to chat with you about the idea of adopting or "building" a personalized parent. One of the definitions for *parent* in the Merriam-Webster dictionary is "the material or source from which something is derived." We need to intentionally Frankenstein a web of mentors and leaders that can be a source for us to derive our mindset, qualities, and success from– a "parent." A well-selected web of minds that become a source for our growth and success.

We can choose whose ideas, mindset, actions, and behavior we incorporate into our own lives, who we want to be an extension of. Of course, one of those sources can be our biological parents if we choose, but it can also be personal mentors, thought leaders, philosophers, and anyone else we'd like to emulate or be inspired by. Choosing who we will be the figurative "child" of allows us to live a more intentional and personally aligned life. World-famous Roman philosopher

Seneca is also a supporter of the Build-A-Parent Workshop. Here is his testimonial:

"We are in the habit of saying that it was not in our power to choose the parents who were allotted to us, that they were given to us by chance. But we can choose whose children we would like to be. There are households of the noblest intellects: choose the one into which you wish to be adopted, and you will inherit not only their name but their [intellectual] property too . . . [those] who wish to have daily as their closest friends Zeno, Pythagoras, Democritus and all the other high priests of liberal studies, and Aristotle and Theophrastus . . . None of them will exhaust your years, but each will contribute his years to yours . . . [he who choose a to be a child of people that inspire them] will have friends whose advice he can ask on the most important or the most trivial matters, whom he can consult daily about himself, who will tell him the truth without insulting him and praise him without flattery, who will offer him a pattern on which to model himself."

## What Does This Mean to You?

If you want to be a really good leader, success, or just live a happier life, be a really good follower first. Religiously consume the content of those you want to be like. Adopt them as your parents, aka people you can learn from and fashion your qualities after. Consult them for advice. "What would ____ do in this situation?" Of course, you can't adopt all these leaders or inspirations into a traditional parent relationship; seeing them every day, creating a strong emotional bond, or even meeting them in person. I'm saying they can become a source of the content that you consume to help shape who you become.

You need to choose your parents ASAP. Everyone successful I've ever known or read about has a network of mentors. I know a lot of coaches. Business, life, mindset, and productivity coaches, and I know even coaches need coaches. No one is so smart that they don't need intentionally chosen mentors.

- Plato mentored Aristotle
- Maya Angelou mentored Oprah Winfrey
- Tony Stark mentored Peter Parker

*Everyone* needs a mentor. But don't stop at one mentor, we urge you to Frankenstein the parent you create in our workshop. As I mentioned earlier, I want your adoptive parent, or the people you source your ideals and beliefs from, to be a web, not one individual. A mesh of people and ideas. Pull from many sources.

Now it's easy for me to say, "just build a web of mentors, duh." How do you do that? Here are ten ways you can help pool together amazing people to become an extension of. I've used every single one of these methods and boy do I have a pretty dope web of parents. Shoutout to all the parents in my life, love you guys. The parents, or people I fashion my mindset after, that know me and don't know me, thank you for changing my life.

## 10 Ways to Add More Sources to Your Intentionally Manufactured Parent Web

### 1. Cold Email

If you aren't familiar with the term "cold email" it just means emailing someone you've had no prior contact with, similar to cold calling. *Do not* underestimate the power of a cold email, especially as a high school or college student. I single out students here because most established professionals or leaders are excited to help up-and-coming students. Being a student is a big foot-in-the-door benefit when it comes to cold emailing. On that note, cold emailing has changed my life. I've booked world-recognized speakers and multi-million-dollar business owners for my podcast via cold email.

If you read a book you love, find the author's email and email them. Tell them how it impacted you. If you see an IG post that really resonates, email them (or DM). If you know someone in your community you'd love to be mentored by, email them. If you don't ask, the answer will always be no.

Cold email Tip: Give them a reason to want to mentor or talk with you. How can you add value to their lives? Do you have an idea or skill that would be of value to them? Get creative. Try to come off as an opportunity for them, not a charity case. *You are valuable,* so act like it. If you do that, you'll have a much better response rate.

### 2. Start a Podcast

Yes, I'd been a podcast junkie for years prior to starting my podcast, and yes, I absolutely love meeting new people. But another reason I started my podcast was to get in a room with people I wouldn't be able to get into a room with otherwise. I'm supplying a new audience for them to reach, and I'm creating positive hype around their mission. That is the value. If you want to have a fifteen to sixty minute conversation with someone who inspires you, a podcast is a great way to make it mutually beneficial for them.

### 3. Go to More Events

Cold emailing is great, but getting yourself face-to-face with people, that's even better. Before I moved to San Diego, I scanned Google, Facebook, Instagram, and Eventbrite for events that would attract successful people I wanted to be like. Some of these events cost money, but it is a 10/10 investment for the sake of achieving your goals. I still do this often. Find events in your area that will put you in a room with inspiring people and talk to as many people at the event as possible. Doing this will change your life and will be super fun!

### 4. Say Hello More

Say hello to people on the elevator. Say hello to people in line with you. Say hello to the person who is smashed up next to you at a concert. I know it can feel awkward at first but do it. You'd be surprised by some of the outcomes of those short conversations.

Talking to Strangers Tip: You get to ask two questions. If they don't ask a question back or seem really engaged after two questions, stop talking. They probably don't want to talk to you.

### 5. What Does Your Friend Group Look like?

Your friends automatically upload to your parent database or web. You will derive facets of your personality and mindset from your friends 100 percent of the time. That doesn't mean all your friends need to be exactly like you and they shouldn't be. My question to you would be: Do they fuel you? Do you encourage and support each other? Do you learn from each other?

### 6. Help Others Get Connected

Be a community builder. If two people you know could benefit from knowing each other, connect them. It takes very little effort to make a group chat introducing two people to each other and that simple favor could change someone else's life. That's cool. If you connect with other people, people will want to help you get connected.

### 7. Read. Read. Read.

Most of the greatest leaders, activists, and creatives ever were diligent self-educators. I am not a reader by nature, although a lot of people think I am. I'm not. In 2021, I went from reading maybe five books a year to reading one to two every week. I don't think I'll do this for the rest of my life, but it was a really cool experience to push myself. It was also cool because it gave me a bit of a theme for each week based on what book I was reading. A lot of books will teach you about people you might want as a parent and give you a deep dive into the author's mindset and personality. Reading books gives you an angle of providing value for people as well –book recommendations. As I mentioned, you don't have to know someone to adopt them as a parent. If you resonate with someone's values or ideas, study the content they put out into the world, and books are a great place to start.

### 9. Take Group Courses

I take a lot of online courses to develop my skills. I particularly love group courses. Growing alongside people, all of you being parented together over some time, is powerful. Group courses can also put you in a room of amazing people with similar goals to yours. Be an initiator. Talk to people in those courses.

### 10. Make Content on a Social Platform

I've made some *amazing* friends and mentors because of the content I put out on social media. TikTok is currently my space of choice, but pick your platform and roll with it. I think the two most underrated platforms for young people like us to create on are LinkedIn and TikTok, but I'm a bit biased. Creating content can bring a lot of cool people into your life.

### 11. Bring the Energy You Want to Receive

In your day-to-day life, emit the energy you want the Universe to emit back. When you walk into a room with high and attractive energy, people notice. If you radiate light, people will naturally be attracted to your presence. Be an attractor.

I'd highly recommend you put at least one of these things I've mentioned into practice. It could change your life. If you haven't adopted parents into your life, do it. Find people who you want to be like and use their knowledge to propel you forward. In our teens or twenties, we are in a very important process of creating our life and mindset. It's important for us to be intentional about what sources we are becoming an extension of.

P.S. Don't forget to be a parent to others who don't know what you know. If you want to receive, give first.

# 17

# I Did What You Said I Was Supposed To, Livi, and I Still Feel like Crap

As we move from part two to part three, I have one more thing that I want to leave you with. Increasing the quality of your state of "being" is all about personal growth, improving emotional intelligence, healing, and increasing mindfulness. Now the deal is, once you start internalizing and incorporating these things into your life, things will change. I want to make sure you are aware of and prepared for that change. No one told me, so I want to bring it to your attention.

I just recently finished watching the Netflix series *Schitt's Creek*. Don't come for me if you are a Rose family lover – I liked it, but I didn't love it. I'm a *New Girl* fan, sue me.

If you aren't familiar with *Schitt's Creek,* it's basically about a family of four, the Rose family, that gets screwed over and loses their fortune and millions and millions in assets. They all lose their status, their "friends," and their jobs. The only asset they have left is a town called Schitt's Creek that the dad, Johnny Rose, bought years earlier as a joke. The family has to move to Schitt's Creek and live in a busted and dusted old motel. They go from billionaires to borderline homeless. As the story arc goes, they hate it there, and then the town adopts them as their own. The Rose family gains perspective, new friends, new businesses, new lovers, and starts living a life that fills them with joy.

What I want to point out about this story is that as you grow as a person and improve your state of being, you will be forced out of your current house. You will be forced from what is comfortable to what is uncertain. You will begin to value yourself, your time, and your energy, and some people won't like that. Oftentimes you will lose friends or the dynamic of your friendships might change, just like the Roses' did. You'll start to lose understanding of who you are because you won't identify with half your labels anymore, just like the Roses did. You might lose a job or a certain status, just like the Roses did. You'll probably go from your comfortable life to a lonely, dusty motel, or a state of feeling lost and in pain for a moment. But you are resilient, and you'll realize, yes, my life was comfortable before, but was I really happy? No. Was I the truest form of myself? No. Your old life will crumble, just like the Roses' did, and a new life and state of being will begin to emerge.

If you decide, and I hope you do, to put in the work to improve yourself, one thing you must know is this: If you do all the things everyone says you are supposed to do – you go to therapy, you start meditating or journaling, you might start taking medication, you remove destructive people and situations, you adopt mindfulness practices, and you work on healing – you might still feel like shit after.

That's normal. Why? You just caused *massive* disruptions to your mindset, life, and your old way of doing things. When you change your state of being, your old self, that version of you that your life was founded on, completely crumbles, and a lot of your old life will go with it. The healthy areas of that foundation will remain, but there will be a lot of rubble to clean up. If you've done what you needed to do and you still feel like shit, it means it's now time for you to rebuild. You deconstructed everything you knew, which is incredibly brave, and now you are in a state of rebuilding. Change is uncomfortable. Stay courageous in that rebuilding process, and I know you will find peace

When we change the way we think and interact with the world, our minds get flipped upside down at a neurological level. As you adjust your mental and physical habits and daily routines from unhealthy to healthy, your brain will begin to physically rewire. Joe Dispenza's *You Are the Placebo* explains this *so* well. This book is one of my personal favorites; it's *fascinating*. Since I can't include the entirety of chapter three of his book here, I'll do my best to give you a very simplified version of the neuroscience he shares (in my own terms).

For years you've done many of the same things every week. You hang out with the same people. You go to the same places. You constantly find yourself at the mercy of the same bad habits. Many of the same insecurities run through your mind. The same things trigger anger or anxiety for you, and the way you deal or don't deal with your emotions is probably fairly consistent. As you've created these routines, your brain started to physically mold to these patterns.

As I mentioned way back in the introduction, the more you do certain things and create certain habits, the more your brain fires those specific neurotransmitters, the body's chemical messengers. The more certain neurotransmitters are fired based on what we do in our daily life, the more ingrained the neural pathways that those messengers take become.

To add to this concept, these neural pathways we have ingrained into our minds become our mental software. We interact with the world and ourselves based on this software. Because of this, naturally, many of us are acting, reacting, and thinking in the past, because we are using the same software that was built by our past experiences. That's what living in the past feels like.

When we begin to change how we think and act daily and no longer act like our past selves, we throw our brains for a loop. We are suddenly using different neural pathways that our brain isn't used to using. That's uncomfortable for your brain, not just for you. Your brain is physically uncomfortable.

This is similar to weightlifting. If you've seen the movie *The Incredibles*, you know Mr. Incredible, or Bob, is clearly skipping leg day. That man is incredibly disproportional. *Incredibly,* hah, pun intended. I can imagine that Bob's arms have gotten very used to doing push-ups and dumbbell curls. His arms probably don't get too sore anymore because they've gotten used to working those muscles. If Bob suddenly started doing an hour of squats and Bulgarian splits every day, he would probably get *really, really* sore.

The same thing goes for how we use our brains. If you used to always be very reactive to other people and suddenly you start becoming very conscious about your reactions and working to stay calm and valuing where you expend your energy, your brain will not feel comfortable doing that for you at first. It's got to trailblaze and work out whole new neural pathways for you. Your conscious mind is now trying to work completely against your body's downloaded software created from your past. Not only is this hard, but it's also really uncomfortable, as I mentioned. As we change our internal software, our body struggles to recognize itself. We momentarily lose who we are. Our old self has crumbled, and our new self is under construction, so we feel very partial and incomplete for a time.

So, you've picked up this book, you are clearly on a personal growth journey. That is only a start. Once you internalize and begin to practice what I teach in this book you've stepped into that rushing river of change, but now you don't get to ride a current, you've got to battle upstream.

By the time we're thirty-five, 90 to 95 percent of who we are is a set of memorized behaviors, skills, emotional reactions, beliefs, perceptions, and attitudes that function like a subconscious automatic computer program.

Using that math, this means by thirty-five only 5 percent of your brain is working consciously. The other 95 percent-ish is working subconsciously or unconsciously. To change, we have to return back to mindfulness. To return back to mindfulness, we've got to use that little 5 percent of conscious thought to convince the other 95 percent, or at least some of it, to become conscious again.

For you, since you're reading this, you've started 5, 10, 15 years before this statistic (35 years old), so it will be a bit easier because you've got a larger amount of developing, conscious brain available to work with. Stuff hasn't become quite as ingrained yet, so ballpark, we'll say you are maybe working at 30 percent conscious brain. That's still not easy and will no doubt feel like a bit of a swim upstream for anyone.

Your mind and body are working in opposition when you first start changing your state of being. But, as you work, it will become 30 percent conscious versus 70 percent subconscious, then 50 percent versus 50 percent, and you will slowly become a more conscious person who is no longer living on autopilot. When you stop living on autopilot, the life you've created on autopilot will collapse because we are moving from a reality that's engineered by our past to creating a better future for ourselves engineered by our conscious, present self.

This is why we feel like shit even after we start making changes. Our body is rewiring. Our brain physically can't even figure out what the hell is going on. We are in the process of rebuilding. If you can stay consistent, you won't have to swim upstream forever. Your life will not feel like it's crumbled forever. You will rebuild and have the life you deserve.

Lastly, it's important to remember that things usually get really bad before they get good. DO NOT GIVE UP. IF YOU CARE DEEPLY ABOUT SOMETHING, PLEASE DO NOT GIVE UP.

During the process of writing this book and starting my own business, there was one specific moment where I seriously considered quitting. I was in the shower, and y'all know the dark rabbit holes of thought that the shower can send you down. I felt beat up, exhausted, and extremely confused. I stood there thinking to myself, "What the f@#% am I doing!? I gave up a full-ride scholarship, I moved back home, and now everything is riding on my shoulders. I just completely flipped my life upside down. If I fail, it's on me. I don't know what my next step is, and no one can tell me what it is. I'm *constantly* working, and I don't even know if

I'm doing this right. On top of that, I'm so, so tired, mentally and physically. I'm putting my soul and hundreds of hours into this book that no one is going to read. Am I delusional? Did I just set myself up for failure? Shit."

As I continued to rethink my entire life, I spiraled into overwhelming fear and doubt. The unknown just felt like too much and it was the first time since starting this journey that I truly considered quitting; stop writing my book, delete my podcast, reapply to colleges and jobs, and give up on my goals. It just felt like way too much for me. Then I remembered a quote I'd recently read:

> **"The thing we want the most comes usually when we're just about to give up."**
> **— Paulo Coelho**

As soon as that quote came into my mind, I had a wave of hope and peace wash over me. I thought to myself, "Well, if that's true, something amazing is about to happen." A big smile came onto my face, and I found myself moving from fear of the unknown to being giddy over it, like a kid on Christmas Eve. I learned at that moment that everything is a matter of perspective. Later that month, I started making the most money I'd ever made in my life, had some massive breakthroughs about this book, booked my first personal podcast feature, and had the opportunity to have conversations with some cool people on my podcast, which always fuels me.

Since then, anytime I'm just about to quit and surrender to my fear, I choose to get excited. I use that overwhelming fear in my favor and know that something beautiful is about to come to fruition. That mindset has never failed me.

Remember, if you are in the pursuit of changing your life and you feel an overwhelming urge to give up, something incredible is just around the corner. That fear is a cue for you to start getting extraordinarily excited. The breakthrough you've been waiting for is just around the corner. The Universe wants to work in your favor, trust her.

As my dad always said, "Finish strong."

# PART THREE

# Doing

**N**ow that we've established how to be in a better state of *being*, mentally and emotionally, we have now arrived at destination number three of our journey: *doing*. In Part Three you will learn how this more aligned, emotionally intelligent, and mindful version of yourself can design a life that brings fulfillment and joy. Designing such a life requires taking purposeful action, overcoming our fears & doubts about the future, and expanding our life perspective – I have included stories, practices, and advice to *do* exactly that.

Read on, my friend.

# 18

# Diagnosing CTP (Chronic Transition Phase)

As I write this chapter about transition phases, I'm currently in a bit of one myself. Recently, I decided to move to San Diego from good-ole Utah, the state I grew up in. At this point, I've only been living in San Diego for about six weeks now. I knew nobody when I got here (besides a few "social media or podcast" friends, most of whom I'd never met in person) and had only been here once in my life, so I barely knew what it looked like around here.

From an outsider's perspective, it made absolutely no sense for me to move here. It's more expensive. I work from home, so I can live anywhere. I knew no one. I had no real solid reasoning . . .

So why did I move? Three reasons in order of their weight in the decision-making process:

1. **It Felt Right**: My intuition was telling me to, and I have a very trusting relationship with myself. I

listen to what my heart and mind are trying to tell me even if I don't know why they're telling me this at the time (remember, generally the answers you need are already inside of you). I mixed this with a bit of meditation and chats with God, and in both practices, I felt moved to make this change, which I mentioned in chapter eleven.

2. **Opportunity**: To meet more young people like myself and find new opportunities to help me grow my business and mission in helping people. I also know I probably won't have the chance to do something so drastic forever, so why not now?

3. **Growth**: I believe every person can benefit from moving somewhere where they know no one. It teaches you new lessons about resourcefulness and allows for a bit of a reset, which we all need from time to time. Also, a change in the environment allows you to create new neural pathways and thought processes because you are no longer simply going through the motions, which is great for growth.

The apartment I now live in has a seven-story parking garage, and I am on level six. Driving down or up that parking garage is some of the longest five minutes of my life. First-world problems, I know. It takes *so long,* though. It's a tall and skinny garage, so multiple times a week I feel like a gumball coming out of a gumball machine while simultaneously trying to not get hit by another gumball going thirty miles per hour in the other direction.

I think that feeling of going "Round-and-Round," as 2010 Selena Gomez once said, is fairly common for teens and especially twentysomethings. Just constantly trying to get to the exit of the parking garage so we can get onto the main road. If your life right now feels like a never-ending parking garage you might have caught something I like to call, CTP, or Chronic Transition Phase. Luckily, it's common and curable, so not to worry. It might feel chronic, but it doesn't have to be.

CTP is most commonly caught between the period of legally becoming young adults at eighteen to our mid-twenties. At these stages, we're being introduced to a new world and a different time of life. Regardless, CTP can be caught at any age and lasts longer depending on who has it.

## Cause of CTP

Our early adulthood is a segment of life that comes with a lot of uncertainty, excitement, confusion, and decision-making; it's a wonderful and exciting phase to do some drastic life-designing. This transition phase of life is magical until it becomes chronic. When twentysomethings find themselves lingering in the transition, rarely making any intentional decisions, and wasting away this magnificent time to transform, it goes from a healthy transition phase to a Chronic Transition Phase or CTP. So how do you know if you have CTP?

## Symptoms of CTP

These are the eight symptoms of CTP that seem to be the most common:

- A lack of curiosity or ability to get outside your comfort zone
- Little to no change in your surroundings or peers
- Staying in a job for too long that doesn't contribute

to professional or personal growth
- Staying in a relationship(s) that are unhealthy or have little to no future
- A major fear of failure
- No relative direction, goals, or plan in place
- Poor habits
- A deep lack of self-love

## Treating CTP

The Cure: INTENTIONAL ACTIONS

Everything from part two of this book – creating mindfulness and a healthier and more-aligned mindset – will help treat CTP because it allows for clarity. Being in a better state of "being" will also help you make decisions for internal rather than external validation. So, Step One of treating CTP, is to be in a better state of "being."

More actionable, intentional treatment is listed below. Depending on your symptom(s), there are certain chapters of this book you should probably spend more time with.

- A lack of curiosity or ability to get outside the comfort zone: Chapter 7 & Chapter 20
- Little to no change in surroundings or peers: Chapter 22 & Chapter 16
- Staying in a job for too long that doesn't contribute to personal growth: Chapter 13 & Chapter 15
- Staying in a relationship(s) that are unhealthy or have little to no future: Chapter 14 & Chapter 21
- A major fear of failure: Chapter 19 & Chapter 10

- No relative direction or any sort of plan in place: Chapter 12 & Chapter 17
- Poor habits: Chapter 21 & Chapter 22
- A lack of self-love: Chapter 9, Chapter 11, Chapter 15

Take **intentional action** and take some extra time to internalize and take notes on these chapters. It will help get you out of the parking garage and onto the main road towards the life you want to create. Without taking purposeful action, we are pretty much just a balloon in the wind.

I also came up with CTP for two reasons. One, because this never-ending transition phase is so common, and I wanted you to know you weren't alone. Two, because when we put a name to our feelings or circumstances, it becomes more real and tangible and easier to work on.

If you have CTP and feel like you're on a never-ending merry-go-round, here's the last thing I'll say. YOU are not the problem; your mindset is. A couple mindset shifts to get you into a better state of being, and you'll be ready to roll. We have to act on our potential. Treating CTP is all very purposeful. Nothing "just happens" as I'm sure you know. The longer we choose to not treat the symptoms of CTP, the harder they will be to cure.

If you want to get your next leg up and not continue on the CTP merry-go-round, you have to decide to become more intentional and change your life trajectory. I'd highly recommend you do that because if you stay on the merry-go-round for too long, you're gonna throw up.

# 19

# Take the Seat

A story, or mantra more so, that I've lived by since I was fourteen is: "Take the Seat." I have very little recollection of the origin of this story I'm about to relay. All I know is that I read it in a book at fourteen as I sat at a small cafe table in the SLC airport preparing to board my first flight alone. I don't know the name of the book. All I know is that the author was a man. I remember, at the time, considering emailing him after I read his story and never did. If you happen to know who the following story belongs to, feel free to contact me.

The story was about a man who was relatively new on the writing scene. I believe he had just completely flipped around his career path. He didn't know exactly what his plan was but was simply taking it a day at a time. I'm still relatively new at the author game myself, but if I understand correctly, in the "olden days" before the internet (as if this wasn't only like twenty to thirty years ago), to find a publisher or literary agent one popular option was to go to a local convention to showcase your writing or most recent book release. As you sat at your convention booth, you prayed that someone would take an interest.

Imagine an author sitting in a stiff, metal fold-out chair at a table with his latest literary baby lovingly placed on display and a cardboard box with additional copies resting at his feet. Fifteen minutes pass . . . forty-five minutes . . . an hour goes by. To make it worse, his section of the convention is practically deserted. Only a handful of agents or publishers were roaming around. He stares at his book. He stares at the other authors tiredly waiting, and he looks back down at his book. At that moment he decides, "Well, if an opportunity won't come to me, I'll go find one."

He stands up, heaves his box of books under his arm, and starts down the hallway to find where all the publishers and agents are, because they *clearly* aren't here. After walking down the wide hallway, he turns the corner and sees a long line of people, a long line of opportunity. At the end of the line of people, sitting on a raised platform, is one established author signing books, making conversation, and quite literally living *his* dream.

The man notices that on the left-hand side of the author there's an empty desk and chair. He eyes the chair for a minute, his eyes sweeping between the line and the empty chair. He lifts his head, adjusts his shirt, and confidently strides towards the raised platform. One leg in front of the other, he reaches the empty chair and takes a seat. Setting his cardboard box comfortably on the ground, he begins setting up his books on the empty table in front of him.

From his peripheral vision, he notices a security guard walking in his direction. The security guard arrives at his side and before she can speak, he looks up and assuredly says, "Sorry I'm late, had a few unexpected delays on the way over."

The security guard looks at him for a moment, looks down at his books on the table, re-establishes eye contact, and with a smile says, "Glad you could make it," and walks off.

The man lands an agent and publication deal that day and goes on to have outstanding success as an author.

The lesson? Opportunity, generally, doesn't just knock – you have to seek it out. You've gotta build the door. You *create* opportunity. You have to choose to *Take the Seat*.

The difference between this man and all the authors who didn't get signed with an agent that day wasn't talent, experience, or intelligence – it was the ability and courage to take initiative. The courage to take the seat, to meet opportunity half way, is something that gets easier as you exercise that muscle. Deciding that opportunity is available if you look for it, that you are worthy of it, and that you will claim it regardless of your fear is what matters.

The following year, the man pulled up out front outside the same building, for the same convention. Upon his arrival, he was shown to the same raised platform and was placed in the exact spot of the author he decided to take a seat next to the year prior. He scanned the room, the familiar and unfamiliar faces, and smiled. He noticed a recognizable face in particular posted in the corner of the room. It was the security guard! Rising from his chair and stepping off the platform, he approached her. With a heart of gratitude, he said, "You knew I didn't belong at that table, you knew I hadn't actually been running late, why did you let me stay?" She looked at him with a warm smile, laughed, and said, "Because I respected your ability to take a seat at the table anyway. No harm, no foul, right?" She understood that if someone was so willing to claim opportunity, to take a chance, that it was proof that they probably belong there. That, and, why let a perfectly good empty table go to waste, right?

I don't know why that story fills my heart up with light as much as it does. I think it's because as someone who often felt so underestimated growing up, especially at the moment I read that story, the gesture of one security guard taking a moment to see him, to *really* see him, and the gesture of the man taking a chance on the potential he saw in himself, is beautiful. That simple story encapsulates humanity, compassion, love, taking chances, overcoming fear, and the power of one decision. One decision can change your life. And the realization of the power of a single moment is so scary and exciting and powerful. I love it.

I believe that the most sublime, poetic moments are found in snapshots of simplicity.

I hope that story inspires you, as well, to seize those powerful, simple moments. But when these moments present themselves, how do we actually take the seat? First, we need to become mindful of what keeps us from not taking it.

There are two main reasons why we don't take action when opportunity hovers in the distance like a lost balloon, or even when it slaps us in the face: fear and unworthiness.

Let's dive into each one, looking at where and how its roots are planted in our minds.

## Reason #1 that we don't Take the Seat: Fear

When an opportunity arises for us, fear can easily begin to present itself. Why is this? Isn't opportunity something we long for? And now that it's here we're scared of it? This is very similar to our common fear of romantic love. I would say this fear bubbles up from two places:

### *Our fear is caused by <u>Uncertainty</u>*

Fear of uncertainty is created by our desire to control outcomes.

We see an opportunity and the potential for it to turn out amazing, and we plow it down by our fear that it won't work out, so we leave it for someone else to claim. We fear failure, we fear that this opportunity might prove that we aren't good enough just as we feared. On the contrary, we might also fear even more so, the realization that we *are* good enough. That if the opportunity plays out in a positive way, our dreams then move from improbable to possible for us. When that realization strikes, we now must take on responsibility. We are now in charge of the fruition of our potential, we can't let ourselves off the hook. Angela Duckworth, an incredible psychologist and popular author, quotes Friedrich Nietzsche, German philosopher and poet, in her book *Grit:* "With everything perfect, we do not ask how it came to be." Instead, "we rejoice in the present fact as though it came out of the ground by magic."

We'd prefer to believe someone amazing or incredibly skilled came from magic or without extreme effort of repeated mundane tasks. Why?

Because, as Nietzsche said, "our vanity, our self-love results in the cult of the genius. For if we think of genius as something magical, we are not obliged to compare ourselves and find ourselves lacking . . . to call someone divine means: here there is no need to compete."

Essentially what Nietzsche is saying here is that if we choose to mythologize natural talent, it places the rest of us in the clear. We're off the hook from holding ourselves to a standard of ever possibly achieving such skill. It gives us the excuse to remain in the status quo.

When Angela uses these quotes of Nietzsche's, she is

relating it to natural versus cultivated talent, but you can also look at it through the additional lens of opportunity. We fear that if we seize the opportunity that we have caught the eye of and ride its wave of uncertainty, we will find that the people who have accomplished what we dream of were not, or were not just, a result of divinity and genius. They were more so a result of repeated mundane tasks, and not magic. This means that our dreams move from inaccessible to accessible. We will then have to apply this rule to ourselves and take responsibility for our potential, which is riddled with uncertainty in the understanding of how to reach it. It's scary to realize you might not be good enough, but even scarier to realize you are, because at this point, the responsibility of you reaching or not reaching your goal becomes very real and personal.

### *Our fear is caused by Judgment*
Fear of judgment is created by our desire to control external perception.

Our fear of rejection is embedded very deeply. It runs as deep as an ancestral survival instinct, as I stated previously in this book. We feel that if others don't accept us that it is proof that we shouldn't accept ourselves, which is very far from the truth. How someone else perceives you is generally a projection of how they see themselves or the world, it has nothing to do with you.

When it comes to Taking the Seat when opportunity presents itself, fear can often override our courage, but as we become self-aware of that fear, we learn to work in harmony with it. We learn that we can choose to just observe that fear, rather than let it control us. As we continue claiming opportunity despite our feelings of fear the easier and easier it becomes.

## Reason #2 that we don't Take the Seat: Unworthiness

I find our feelings of unworthiness for opportunity and success, although often intertwined with our fear, derive from three spaces:

### 1. Shame

We might shame ourselves out of feeling worthy enough to take advantage of an opportunity because we feel like it makes us ungrateful for what we already have.

There is no shame in wanting more for ourselves. All that means is that you recognize your own potential. If you feel you have the skill or capabilities for a specific opportunity, you don't need to shame yourself out of taking it. It doesn't make you egotistical to recognize that you're a skilled person. If we remain grateful for the present as we look towards the potential of our future, no shame is needed. This shame, in relation to our desire for more, can flow from the river of comparison.

### 2. Comparison

Our constant knack to fall into comparative suffering is soooo bad for us. Basically, comparative suffering means I can't dislike my current life situation because someone else has it worse. Suffering is suffering. Just because someone else is struggling in a different way doesn't make your suffering any less valid. You are entitled to feel tough emotions regardless of the comparative severity of your situation. Validate your experiences and your pain, please! If you feel unhappy or unfulfilled and are seeking opportunity or change, it is completely justifiable.

We also compare via credibility, which results in unworthiness, a.k.a. the over-used phrase: imposter syndrome. Outwardly, someone else seems more qualified to hold the space we are holding, so we feel unworthy. This isn't just professionally, this could also be, for example, a relationship. Comparing ourselves to someone's prior partner and feeling like we aren't as worthy of someone's attention or love. Harsh comparison is a terrible way to determine our worthiness.

### 3. Trauma

Someone else's voice can be planted in our head, reminding us of our unworthiness.

Someone in your past, probably a parent or guardian, made you feel unworthy. Unworthy of success, love, or a beautiful life. If that is the case, if someone in your life made you feel unworthy of your pure desire to fulfill your potential/goals, it's time to heal. Spend some quality time with chapter nine. Someone else who didn't heal has warped your reality. As someone who has your best interest at heart, believe me when I say, *you are worthy.*

Overcoming our fear of uncertainty and our feelings of worthiness is as simple as recognizing it, confronting it, and repeatedly leaning into it. Have you ever seen one of those videos of some person playing with an alligator or lion as if it were a harmless wiener dog? It's similar to that. The more we spend time with our fear the more we become harmonious with it.

A final thought when it comes to seizing the opportunity in our life.

A mentor once said to me that sometimes "we carry our dreams with such a heavy heart, let them be light." What he meant by this is that we long for our dreams with such intensity it can physically ache. I can feel that longing rise up in me as I write this sentence; I get it. But if we let it get too heavy, it paralyzes us. Don't let your hopes for the future kill your ability to enjoy what you love. To enjoy the present.

You don't have to boil the ocean, just work on boiling the water that is currently in your pot.

One day at a time my love.

# 20

# Is Skydiving Actually *That* Scary?

**M**y favorite place I've ever had the opportunity to travel to was New Zealand. I wouldn't consider myself much of a nature freak, and I don't like hiking much, but that place is *magical*. Everything I love in two cute little islands. Alpacas, the best stargazing on the PLANET, great airport bathrooms, cute animals, a lot of places that look like they were built by fairies, nice strangers, the most adorable little shops, very polite road signs (Ex. NZ sign: We love you, so please wear a seatbelt friend – U.S. road sign: If you don't wear a seatbelt you'll f***ing die you idiot), a lot of eco-conscious restaurants, and the most Indiana Jones-esque winding roads ever. Every. Single. Thing. We did. Was fantastic. 100-star Yelp review.

I also got to do a lot of things I'd never done before there. Being the adrenaline junkie I am, one of those things was skydiving. I dragged my mom, a.k.a. my travel buddy, onto a tiny airplane with glass floors thousands of feet in the air. Just before we walked inside to get the skydiving day started, she asked if I'd Googled their safety reports when I booked it. I hadn't, so I did a quick search. Turns out a plane of theirs had crashed into the water a month prior. Nobody died or got seriously injured, and they said it was a freak accident, so I figured it probably wasn't worth noting to my mom. Like the awesome daughter I am, I lied and told her it looked like they had great safety records, nothing to worry about. We went inside, watched a quick video, strapped on our parachutes, and packed onto the plane. She cried on the plane, and I helped her laugh through the fear. Then we jumped out, well, technically bum scooted. Our instructor had us swing our legs out over the edge, dangling in the wind like noodles, and then you just get sorta swept away, like a hat flying out a window on the freeway.

The deal with skydiving is that it doesn't feel at all how I expected. The world always made it seem so scary and chaotic. It's not that scary, and it's not very chaotic. Even my mom agreed, and that woman is *not* an adrenaline junkie. You fall for about forty-five to sixty seconds, and it's so fast that your brain doesn't even register what's happening. After sixty seconds, you pull the chute and you come to a slow, calm float. It's surprisingly peaceful. We went just as the sun was setting over the water, so it was also gorgeous. Then you gently slide into the grass and it's over. No crazy adrenaline rush, mainly because your brain doesn't know it's falling because you have no perception of how far you are from the ground like you do on a big roller coaster drop. Skydiving is more serene than anything else.

What I've found is that making bold changes in your life isn't as scary and chaotic as the world makes it out to be. Why? Because the majority of the world never decides to get bold. Just like the majority of the world has never been skydiving. So, all these people that say skydiving is so scary and give it that reputation, have never been. They've never actually jumped. It might be scary in the plane as you build up the courage to make the change, but once you jump, it's usually pretty peaceful.

Quitting a job you hate feels scary, but if it feels right, it brings more peace than chaos. Same with ending a bad relationship, deciding to change majors, deciding to dress differently, coming out to your parents, moving states, starting a business . . . It's scary, but if it feels like what you need to be truly aligned as a person, jump. Do it.

When I dropped out of college to rewrite my life, including writing this book, moving to San Diego, running my podcast, and starting my business, I was scared, but I knew it felt right, so I did it. And surprise, surprise, I'm the happiest I've ever been. It was peaceful after the jump. Yes, I often feel like I have a lot on my plate, and it gets pretty stressful, but it's the type of thing I'm willing to get stressed for. Now I get stressed because I care. I get the good type of stress now instead of getting stressed because I've got to work another shift or take another test that I strongly dislike.

As we make big, bold decisions, it's still important that we address our fear. I feel fear about my life all the time. We don't need to be fearless, because it *is* scary to swing our legs over the edge of that plane. To look at that big life decision in the face. I won't act like it's not and that we should all just toughen up. If you want to cry on the plane, you cry on that frickin plane! No shame. Fear of failure and fear of making the "wrong" life decisions is very real. It's a part of the human experience. We aren't trying to get rid of that fear and anxiety, what we want to work towards doing is being at peace with it. Stop fighting so hard. You don't need to.

The constant worrying, overthinking, stressing, wrestling, grappling, pleading, yearning, sobbing, thrashing . . . It's KILLING you. Stop it.

Let yourself breathe. Let your shoulders drop. Let your jaw unclench. Let your muscles relax.  Let life ebb and flow and allow yourself to ebb and flow with it. You don't always have to feel okay. Your life doesn't always have to be working out or else you're failing. It's okay for things to not be okay for the moment. Surrender to it. You don't need to be a fighter all the time. When you surrender to life instead of fighting it all the time, that's what peace feels like. After we give ourselves a moment on the ground to restore our energy bar from red to green, accept our scars and learn, we get back up and push on.

That being said, as you make all these tough decisions – college, money, moving out, marriage, kids, career, finance management – the goal is to find peace in the uncertainty because life will always be uncertain. That's never going away. Jonathan Field put it best on his podcast: "to find the capacity for equanimity in the face of sustained uncertainty."

How do we find peace amongst the chaos of our lives? How do we find peace in the doing? How do we become stronger than fear and allow ourselves to jump into bold decisions? We become truly present. That's what part two is all about. But there are two culprits that can override our ability to have peace, to be present: fear and anxiety.

As humans, our typical reaction to fear and anxiety is to get rid of them as soon as possible. To fight them. As I mentioned, this constant fighting is exhausting. What we need to do is feel them, as I mentioned in my chapter about healing.

In a recent talk I gave to a large group of college students about healing, I talked about needing to feel our emotions. The only way to truly release ourselves from the pressure painful emotions can have on our mental state is to feel the emotions. Write about them. Talk about them. Accept them. Learn from them.

One woman, also in her early twenties, came up to me after my talk and asked an awesome question, "Why? Why do I need to feel my anxiety and fear? I don't get it." I'm so happy she asked me that because now I can share the answer I gave to her, with you.

I mentioned the answer briefly in a prior chapter, but let's go deeper here. When anxiety, fear, and any other distressing feelings emerge, our bodies are trying to send us a signal. Your body's main goal is to survive. When life gets overly uncertain, your mind feels like you're in danger. It starts saying, "If you fail, it's game over. No coming back from a screw up like that," or, "You don't know exactly what you're going to do next? Great, we're screwed."

Your brain is trying to be helpful and keep you safe from pain or distress. If we refuse to listen to her, she'll keep hitting the anxiety or fear button until we do. She'll keep setting off alarms until we choose to acknowledge and hear them. The key to becoming harmonious with your mind is to tell her that you hear her. Feel those emotions. Acknowledge the alarms. That's all she wants you to do. Be still and say: "I hear you."

## How to Let Yourself Feel Your Unpleasant Emotions

### Step One: Be Still

A lot of times when we get anxious, whether you have anxiety like me or get anxious from thinking about your future, our instant reaction is to take action. Find a way to push down, remove, or distract ourselves from the anxiety or fear. We think, "Let me just play guitar, let me just go for a drive, let me just play with my dog, let me just take a nap, let me just keep my mind busy and it will go away." Sometimes trying to find an external fix for what you're feeling is not the best course of action. Sometimes you need to have the courage to just sit in it and feel it. That's usually the quickest way for you to rid yourself of that unpleasant anxious feeling. When you just make your mind busy, you're bandaging the issue. Not healing it. Sit in your emotions, meditate, sit in silence, go on a quiet walk; let yourself just feel for a moment. No external input.

### Step Two: Thought Separation

Once you can find a place to be still and quiet, take some deep breaths. Big inhale, long exhale. Now think of your anxious thoughts and feelings like a raging waterfall. If you are standing under that heavy, crashing waterfall, you'll be cold, in pain, and super uncomfortable. If you can step behind the waterfall and watch it fall in front of you, it's much more comfortable. Focus on your rushing thoughts and feelings and do your best to perceive them as a separation of you. You are the conscious thought, and these unpleasant feelings are the subconscious looking back at you. You may have heard the famous quote: "You are not your thoughts; you are the observer of your thoughts." Get behind that waterfall and observe it. Don't try to stop it or understand it, just observe, like watching cars rush back and forth on a freeway as I mentioned in the meditation chapter.  This is one of the cores of mindfulness, removing reactive actions and instead taking moments to observe our feelings from a third person perspective. If we create space, we create clarity.

### Step Three: Talk to your body

Now that you feel still and have begun to outwardly observe the thoughts that your body is generating, talk to them. It might sound a bit odd or childish, but holy crap does it work! We have slowed our breathing, external stimulation, and the intensity of our anxiety at this point. Now, close your eyes and tell your body and mind that you hear her. Tell your anxious body "I hear you. Thank you for trying to protect me. I appreciate you for wanting me safe. Right now, everything's okay. I don't need these warnings you're sending. I hear you. I hear you. I hear you."  You can say these things out loud or in your mind.

Do this while taking deep, steady breaths. At this moment, you can also place both hands on your chest, one on top of the other. Apply slight pressure and allow the warmth of your hand to fill your chest. You are giving your body a hug. Your inner child gets scared, anxious, and frightened. Nurture her. Nurture yourself.

I swear by these exercises I've shared with you. They might sound odd and very foreign, but I promise they help. Try them next time you feel overwhelmed by life. As you enter these big moments and decisions of your life, don't forget to hug yourself, be loving towards yourself, and give your body and mind the space to talk to you. It will make you feel a lot better in the present and will give you a lot of clarity about your future.

Staying mindful and emotionally aware will be the air that fills your parachute as you jump into new chapters of your life. These practices I shared have the power to transform a chaotic freefall into a peaceful, pleasant experience. Give yourself the gift of peace. Fill your parachute with air.

# 21

# A Big Ole Pile of Perspective

**W**e reached the bottom of the Utah mountain at 5:00 am and headed to the trailhead. It was expected to be a seven-hour hike round trip. We got to the mountain as early as possible because it was supposed to be pretty hot that day, somewhere in the mid to high 90s, which is fairly uncommon for Utah weather in September.

We hiked at a steady pace, and I was extremely out of breath and definitely complained the most. Hear me out, though, the entire thing was a scramble up rocks, no nice clear path, and basically all up-hill switchbacks. PLUS, I was hiking with three avid hikers and climbers! Now that I'm trying to plead my case, looking back I was probably being kind of a wussy, but any Utahn would agree that it's not an easy hike. We finally made it to the top, and I will say, it was the prettiest view I've probably ever seen in Salt Lake County.

After thirty to forty-five minutes we headed back down. It was probably about 9:30 am at this point. Considering the trail was steep and rocky the whole way down, you really had to watch your step. My two friends who moved like mountain goats had a somewhat easy time navigating the rocky path. A friend and I decided we wanted to move a little slower, so we stuck together with a few switchbacks behind our other two friends up ahead. After about fifteen minutes downhill, an incident occurred. The crappy, old, pink Nikes I decided to wear, for what reason I don't know because they had absolutely no tread, failed me. My foot slipped off the edge of a rock I had stepped on and bent just the wrong way. Snap. My leg broke all the way through one bone and halfway through the other just above the ankle. How it broke *that bad* just by taking one bad step, I have no idea.

Long story short, it took about seven hours for us to get down the mountain with the help of search and rescue. It ended up in the news, and I got to spend many lovely, long, excruciating hours at the ER.

Fast forward after two weeks of no sleep (cause: pain), no bowel movements (cause: surgery drugs), a lot of Percocet, and seven screws and a rod in my leg, I headed back to my college campus on my little leg scooter decked out with dollar store butterfly stickers. I also threw away my pink Nikes and haven't gone hiking since.

One day I was headed up campus from my business philosophy class and it started pouring rain. My campus was built on a hill, so scooting up to my dorm took almost triple the time. I didn't have an umbrella on me, so I slowly scooted on my butterfly scooter in the rain toward my dorm room. I felt really bummed and irritated. At that moment I remember looking up and a big smile came onto my face. I watched all these fellow irritated, soaked college students rushing towards their classes getting drenched around me unable to do anything about it; we all looked like dorks. If you took a second look at the situation it was actually pretty funny. We all looked so grumpy and sad; it was hilarious. Well, if you find minimal human misery hilarious, I thought it was funny. I made it to my building really wet, but in a really good mood.

For whatever reason, I think about that moment a lot. In that very simple moment, Mother Nature ingrained the importance of perspective into my mind. Our reality is whatever we perceive it to be. *Everything* is perspective.

We get so worked up over minor inconveniences: snarky comments, that one annoying co-worker, someone cutting us off on the freeway, all these little things that don't even matter. One person was rude to you at the gym, and you spend the rest of the day telling every person you interact with about that single rude comment. What a **massive** waste of energy.

One question that is constantly at the top of my mind and has completely changed the way I live: is this *really* worth expending my limited energy?

We love to fall into the victim stance; we love to expend our energy on the minor inconveniences. Stop it. It is ruining your life. That is not an exaggeration. Constantly spending your energy on things that won't matter in a week, a month, a year, will destroy the joy and beauty that daily life is full of if you choose to perceive it that way. When you work on being present and valuing yourself, you will begin to feel the daily inconveniences becoming less inconvenient. Was your roommate or sister stealing your shirt actually that big of a deal to expend a bunch of energy over? Was that unnecessary comment your friend made yesterday really worth gossiping about with your partner for three hours? Was that one bad moment at work really worth ruining your whole day? Was Taco Bell getting your order wrong really worth getting angry over? Most of the time, the answer is no.

We only have so much energy in a day, if we want to design a fantastic life, we can't expend our energy on all this stupid shit. We need that energy for other, more important things. Protect it at all costs. Be cautious with your energy expenditure like you are with your money. If anything, protect your energy more than your wallet. Money can be replenished, time and energy come in a finite supply.

It's usually the small things in our daily lives that eat away at us slowly over time, we don't usually find ourselves at rock bottom because of one big inconvenience. It's the slow internal festering. Not only that, if we constantly complain and take the victim stance, we will attract negative energy and repel positive energy. Your reality becomes your perspective of it. Energy is king. Use it wisely.

As we design our lives, learning when we should and shouldn't expand our energy is a skill we must learn. Below are ten questions that will place your perspective on the big picture and help you know where to expend your energy. Choosing one question each day for the next ten days to use as a journal prompt, meditate on, or contemplate, will shift your perspective on your life in at least one way. You will find a new view that puts your life in long-term light, a light that doesn't seem so daunting and confusing.

## Life Perspective Questions

### 1. What do you feel you *should* do with your life, that you don't actually *want* to do?

You feel like you should get a certain major that you completely hate. You feel like you should continue to keep a friend, but they constantly seem to drag you down. You feel like you should stay in your relationship because you've already invested so much time. You feel like you should say yes to a free drink even though you told yourself you weren't going to drink tonight. It's pretty easy to know what we should do, but what do you actually want to do? What you want matters.

We might feel pressure to do something because we feel we should, but that doesn't mean it is necessarily the best thing for us. Even if you feel you *should* do something, if it isn't in alignment for you, don't do it.

### 2. What in my life is truly out of my control that I should no longer continue expending energy on?

The way your parents treat you is out of your control. The way that white Honda Civic drives on the freeway is out of your control. The stupid assignments your professor assigns are out of your control. Yet, we continue to expend frustrated energy over these things. We whine, complain, groan, and ruminate. This exhausts so much mental energy when we could just accept things for what they are and move on with our day.

Daily question to ask yourself: Is this situation or inconvenience out of my control? If the answer is yes, don't expend any more energy trying to change it or complaining about it. Recognize that you feel frustrated and then deal with it. Recognize that you can only control yourself and your mind.

**3. What do I want my life to look like in one year? Five years? Socially? Professionally? Monetarily? Spiritually? Mentally? Physically?**

What do I <u>not</u> want my life to look like in one year and what should I stop doing to avoid that?

**4. What habits need to be broken? Who should I spend less time with? What should you spend more or less time on?**

**5. Where am I overextending myself?**

When it comes to goals, if you try to do everything at once, you won't be able to do anything at all. Sometimes we need to just cut our losses, accept that there is only so much time in a day, and remove some obligations or pursuits in our life.

**6. What are my deepest core values? (choose three to five)**

Examples: honesty, integrity, empathy, simplicity, compassion, resilience, personal alignment, relationship building, compassion, achievement, gratitude, balance, community, growth, knowledge, leadership, organization, loyalty, fun, self-expression, success…

If an opportunity doesn't align with your core values, avoid it.

**7. What is my "why"?**

This can mean something different depending on the context. My why in life, what lights me up, is making ideas manifest in whatever way I see fit. My reason for my business is to highlight the sublimity of each unique person. My reason for this book is to aid people in their ability to live in alignment.

**8. Where am I discounting my achievements?**

**9. What are you a badass at? Regardless of where in your life you think you're failing, what would you five or ten years ago be so proud of you for accomplishing? That's something to celebrate.**

**10. What are my strengths and weaknesses?**
Be honest. Maybe ask someone you trust what they think your strengths and weaknesses are. Be willing to take constructive criticism.

# 22

# The Goalden Rule

The smell of wet paint triggers a lot of nostalgia for me. I'll walk into a public building under construction, and the second that smell hits my nose my brain says, "mmm childhood <3" This nostalgic trigger isn't because I was one of those kids that shoved permanent markers up their nose even though everyone warned them that it would kill their brain cells – gotta love those kids. The house I grew up in was built and general contracted by my mom and dad. I spent a lot of time handing my dad tools up on scaffolding, watching my mom and grandpa do *a lot* of electrician work, hearing about creepy workers hitting on my mom, a lot of lawsuit drama, pulling massive sunflowers from our backyard dirt, playing hide and seek in granite stores with my sister, and of course being around the smell of wet paint. That house took my parents *a while,* so being on a construction site became a part of my child, which was fun. I still have my grandpa's red pocket knife he gave me that I thought was so cool.

Watching this process growing up and hearing more about it later in my life, I developed an interest in architecture, a growing interest in real estate, and big respect for electricians. There were. So. Many. Wires. From what I understand, what often happens in real estate is people want to sell their house for a lot of money but aren't willing to invest their money into getting the house renovated or staged to sell at that higher price. When it comes down to it, homeowners often have two options: you spend more time and money to hopefully make even more money or get the sale over with and hopefully break even. Investing for a higher payoff scares people, and reasonably so – who knows if that investment will have the expected payout? Uncertainty and the unknown are a tough space to find peace in.

Whether people decide to renovate their house before selling it is beside the point. What I'm getting at is the importance of investing in yourself and how that will get you much higher returns in life. The investment and those returns could be money, joy, relationships, or achievement.

I am a big believer in the power of prep work and investing in yourself. We can't bank on people investing in us, we have to invest in ourselves, believe in ourselves, and lean into uncertainty. Choosing to invest in yourself will be one of the best choices you ever make. One of the best ways you can invest in yourself is with time. Specifically, taking time to get clear on your goals, how you will achieve them, and what systems and habits you will need to put in place for yourself to make it happen. There is a beautiful art to prep work, and if done correctly, it will bring a lot of fulfillment and achievement.

> **"Give me six hours to chop down a tree and
> I will spend the first four sharpening the ax."**
> **— Abraham Lincoln**

Prep work is the name of the game, just like Abe says. For example, I spent *way* more time planning, outlining, and doing research for this book than actually writing it and most authors can attest to that as well. Why did I devote a chapter of my book to prep work and goal setting?

Because as you go ahead in your life and strive to achieve the things you feel passionate about, your motivation will not be the determining factor of your success; the systems and structure you put in place for yourself will be.

**"You do not rise to the level of your goals; you fall to the level of your systems"**
**— James Clear**

These systems are mental and physical. If you want achievement, you need positive systems and habits that can make that happen. You've probably heard of the Clifton Strengths test, which is an online tool to help you figure out where you are exceptional and naturally talented. I think it's a great tool to start improving self-awareness. After taking a twenty-minute test, it tells you your top strengths.

My #1 strength? Strategy. I'm a strategy nut because I know how much it matters. (I also have anxiety, so it helps me feel more at ease haha) Due to my strategy nuttiness, I've tried *a lot* of goal setting and habit building systems and I want to share with you what has worked for me. If it resonates with you, I'd love for you to try to adopt one of these systems I use into your life.

Before setting goals to achieve the things we desire to achieve, we need to first ask ourselves **what** those goals are and **why** we even want to achieve them?

## What Are Your Goals?

Let's talk about purpose. A million people every day are asking themselves, "What's my purpose?" I can answer that for you. In my mind, everyone's purpose is the same. To learn and progress as a human being via new experiences and adversity. Life is about growth and learning, that's it. If you're doing that, you're fulfilling your purpose. What I think people mean when they ask that question is "How can I best live my life to receive the most fulfillment and joy?" That's a tougher question to answer. This is how you can begin to answer that question. Try as many things at the buffet as possible. You have no way to know what will fulfill you the most in life if you aren't trying different options. Curiosity, that's the key. Stop trying to find your purpose and instead just be curious. If you're not getting uncomfortable through new experiences consistently, you aren't being curious enough. Get curious, sample a lot of options at the buffet life has to offer. Some dishes you'll like more than others, but eventually, you'll try a really good buffet option and say, "Wow, I love this. I could devote a lot of time to this." Stop eating the same thing every time you go to the buffet, *especially* if you don't like it that much. Load up that buffet plate baby and if you don't like some of the things you try, throw it out. You're now one step closer to finding the things at the buffet that make you the happiest and most fulfilled. That's how you live a fulfilling life. Throw out the word purpose and invest time into getting curious.

## Why do you want to achieve those goals?

Along with that, sometimes we don't stop and question why we are pursuing certain things. Why do we keep eating a certain buffet food? Why are you setting these certain goals? Ask yourself if your "why" for doing something is healthy, sustainable, and fulfilling. Are you trying to achieve these goals for the right reasons? Reasons that will contribute to your happiness and ability to live a good life.

*Example:*
Goal: Graduate with a law degree.

Why do I want to graduate with a law degree? To make a lot of money.

Why do I want to make a lot of money? Because I want to buy cool stuff that I could never buy before.

Why do I desire so strongly to buy all the things I could never buy before? If I have a cooler house, car, clothes . . . people will like me more.

Why do I want people to like me more? Growing up I always felt insecure about whether people liked me.

Why did I feel so insecure about being like this? Because my parents rarely expressed their love for me.

Childhood trauma is not a good reason to get a law degree. It's healing time, not law degree time.

If you ask yourself "Why?" enough times, you'll get to the core of why you want to achieve certain things. Make sure that "why" positively aligns with who you are and want to be.

Occasionally, I've found *myself* pursuing certain things out of spite because I hated being underestimated and I wanted to prove myself. For example, I told myself "Once I make a lot of money, I'll buy myself a dope car, and then everyone will stop underestimating me." I took a step back and thought to myself "Why would I do that? I don't even like fancy cars that much?" So… that's no longer a goal of mine because I don't need to prove shit! I especially don't need to spend a bunch of money to prove shit. YOU don't need to prove shit to *anyone*. You're in the pursuit of living your most joyful and fulfilling life not to prove a bunch of people wrong who don't have your best interest in mind. Check yourself. Is your why coming from a place of self-love? Of course, people doubting you can be a motivator but don't let it become your why. Achieve success because you love yourself and you love the people you surround yourself with. Money, spite, anger, fear, or because someone else is telling you to live your life a certain way are not healthy "whys". Ask, does this thing I'm pursuing ring true to my values and who I want to be? If the answer is yes, go for it. If you realize it's an unaligned goal, stop.

Now that we've talked about knowing our reason for achieving certain things, let's get to the achievement portion. Strategy and structure. Before you create a physical structure, you must create a mental structure to achieve your goals. Of course, everything I've shared in part two will improve your mental structure, but I still want to touch on this here: The #1 rule for achieving your goals, the Goalden Rule.

## The Goalden Rule: Your words and thoughts matter.

The things we think and say create our reality. What comes out of your mouth and what goes on in your head will shape your life. Adjust what you think and what you say, and you will have a much higher chance of achieving your goals.

Do you want to be in a healthy relationship? Stop saying and thinking, "Women are confusing, and I'll never understand them," or "All men suck," or "I just suck at relationships, and I always will."

Do you want to make more money? Stop saying and thinking, "I'll always be broke," or "I'll never be able to afford that."

When you say these things, you are solidifying that reality in your mind. Your mind is the creator of your reality. What you think and say frequently, is what your life becomes. Change your thoughts and words to:

"I am preparing to meet an amazing person and enter a healthy relationship."

"I will no longer let my pain hold me back from receiving love."

"How can I figure out a way to afford that thing I've always wanted to buy?"

"I don't have a lot of money now, but I know that money is abundant, and I will find a way to attract it into my life."

Your words and thoughts matter. Be conscious about them. Pay attention to what you say out loud and what you constantly think in your mind. Those two things are creating your reality. Shift the way you speak to others and yourself about your goals.

To start shifting your thoughts I want you to write three of your goals down. Example:

1. Fully support myself with my art.
2. Have a great group of friends.
3. Buy my dream apartment.

Now convert them into "I have" statements:

1. I can fully support myself through my art commissions.
2. I have an amazing group of supportive friends.
3. I have the apartment of my dreams.

Take this one step further and convert these into "I am" statements. What type of person would you need to be to have these things?

1. I am someone that has a valuable skill that people are willing to invest in.
2. I am someone that attracts high-frequency people.
3. I am living joyfully in the apartment I've worked hard to have.

Write these three "I am" statements on a piece of paper, tape them on your mirror, and say them to yourself every morning multiple times. Do the best you can to buy into and believe those three things you say. As you do this your mind will begin to align with the version of you that is those three things and in turn, you will act like that version of you that has achieved those things. There are more levels to the art of manifestation but that's a good one to start with.

Finally, the physical structure of achieving your goals. Time management, goal setting, and daily structure. Let's dive into a few tactical tips that will give you the daily structure needed to carry out your life objectives.

## Simple Tactical, Time Management Tips to Help You Tackle Your Goals

### *1. Figure Out How Long It Actually Takes You to Do Things*
This one was a game changer for me. If you're someone who is late or running behind to a default, this one's for you. I used to be late to *everything*. I realized that I was late all the time because I thought getting dressed and starting a batch of

laundry would take me fifteen minutes when in reality it would take me thirty minutes. My perception of time and how long tasks actually took me was way off. How do you adjust this?

For two to four weeks, every weekday night make yourself a minute-by-minute schedule for the upcoming day. It will allow you to start noticing how long specific tasks actually take you and aid in readjusting your personal time awareness. For example, doing this exercise you might find that you think it takes you forty-five minutes to shower and get ready but really it takes an hour. Our ability to be aware of that is a huge strength when it comes to time management. Here's how a schedule for me might look:

| | Tuesday |
|---|---|
| 7:00 - 7:45 | **Wake up & Get Ready for Gym** |
| 7:00 - 8:00 | **Meditate & Make Bed** |
| 8:00 - 9:00 | **Workout** |
| 9:00 - 9:45 | **Shower & Get Ready** |
| 9:45 - 1:45 | **Book Writing** |
| 1:45 - 3:45 | **Client Work** |
| 3:45 - 4:45 | **Zoom Meeting** |
| 4:45 - 6:45 | **Client Work** |
| 6:45 - 7:45 | **Break** |
| 7:15 - 8:15 | **Laundry + Clean Bathroom** |
| 8:45 - 9:45 | **Read** |
| Sleep by 12 | **Extras: *car wash * send an email to ___** |

There are a few things about this schedule I want to point out:

- 45 minutes to wake up, brush my teeth, wash my face, and throw on some leggings might seem like way too big of a time chunk. I've tried telling myself this takes me 15 minutes, but it *never* does. It's 30-45 minutes every time. Something about the slow morning I just can't seem to move much faster . . . so I account for it. I learned how long this actually took me.
- I also have a 4-hour book writing chunk. I, personally, can sit down for 3 or 4 hours, lock in, and write; however, someone else might learn that they can't do that. If you don't prefer to do that, break your work or study time down into smaller chunks.
- You also might notice I don't have time to eat added in. For one thing, I'm a meal prepper so I don't need time to make food, all I do is heat it up. I also found trying to schedule in times to eat had me eating when I wasn't hungry yet, so I just eat intuitively throughout the day.
- At the bottom I include extra things to do if I have any free time.
- Lastly, if you try this method, don't be too strict or get stressed about staying on schedule. This is a rough outline for your day that allows for some loose structure. We are not robots and trying to perfectly follow a minute-by-minute schedule every day is not the idea of this structure.

If you like doing this structural time management, feel free to keep doing it. I've been structuring my days out like this for years and it helps me in so many ways. I'm very aware of how long it takes me to do certain tasks now, but also on busy weekdays it allows me to fall asleep at night knowing I used my time as wisely as I could have. I don't usually do it on weekends though; give myself some non-structured time to create or be with loved ones.

## 2. Going 0 to 100 Usually Doesn't Work

Ugh, I so wish this wasn't the case. Life had to teach me this lesson over and over and over. If you're working on creating a new habit – meditating every morning, reading twenty minutes/day, going to the gym three times/wk., working on a skill hr./day, learning how to cook something new once/wk. – allow yourself the space to ease into that habit. Trying to go from never meditating to doing it every day, or rarely working out to going five days/wk. is a lot to ask of yourself. Be gentle with yourself. Even if you go full throttle and start meditating every day, it most likely won't last for more than a few weeks. This doesn't mean you're weak or lack self-control, this failure to keep up after hitting the gas full throttle happens at a neurological level.

As I mentioned earlier in this book, our minds have to physically rewire when we change environments or mindsets; the same goes for habits. Your brain is more likely to rewire with more ease and give long-lasting results when you redirect one wire per day, not when you try to rip out and replace the entire breaker. Ease in.

As you create a habit, keep it just below feeling like straining work, because when a new habit feels too uncomfortable your brain goes, "Oh, this is uncomfortable. Don't do this again." That's the reaction you don't want. But, if you start building the habit of going to the gym everyday by going once or twice per week for twenty minutes, your brain goes, "Hmm, this is new, but the body's telling me it feels good. Maybe this gym thing isn't too bad."

### 3. If You Try to Do Everything at Once, You Won't Be Able to Do Anything at All

If you are someone that doesn't know how you want to spend your time, I hope the advice earlier in this chapter was helpful. If you are someone that's mind cranks out a stack of ideas every day and you get overly ambitious, I'm in your boat. But what I've found is that we really do have to intentionally choose where we direct our focus if we want to achieve any of the goals we set for ourselves. I've tried doing it all at once many times and it usually just brings tears, exhaustion, burnout, lost potential, it can damage relationships, etc. When I first started on this entrepreneurial path, I was running a podcast, taking a book writing course, writing my book, working a part-time job, pursuing modeling and acting, and working on a business startup. I felt like crap, constantly. I was having the worst panic attacks I'd ever experienced and because I was so overwhelmed, I barely enjoyed doing all these things I used to love. So, I dropped modeling and the startup, and amazingly enough, a weight was lifted off my shoulders. My acne cleared up, I stopped having panic attacks, my relationships with loved ones got better. Again, be gentle with yourself. You have time. If you try to go after all your goals at once, you won't be able to accomplish much at all.

### 4. Habit Stacking

This phrase was coined by author Steve Scott. Habit stacking is so simple, but so effective. Habit stacking is stacking a new habit on top of an existing habit. Let me give you examples of how I've used this concept on a personal level. When I first started meditating, I had a very solid habit of making my bed in the morning. Turns out telling myself, "I'll just make time to do it at some point" doesn't work, so I started meditating directly after I finished making my bed. After doing that, I've meditated almost every morning for years since. Occasionally, I get busy or overwhelmed and my daily meditation starts to fall off. I give myself empathy, realign, and restack. I might try stacking mediation to a different morning ritual and go from mediating twenty minutes back down to five and work my way back up. I say this again for me as much as I'm saying it for you, we are not robots. Our habits or routines are not supposed to be perfect.

### 5. Make a Pact

Most of you know that you need to write your goals down and give yourself goal markers or step by step mini goals to reach those, which you *definitely* should do if you haven't. I'd rather use this last tip to talk about something that I don't see mentioned as often, writing down a mindset you want to continue to embody as you work towards achieving your goals. A personal pact. I create a pact with myself at the start of every new year, but you can create one whenever you'd like. This pact is a list of values and overall mindsets you want to stay aligned with. After you write those down, you sign it, and tape it to a mirror or wall where you can see it every day. Almost every day as I get myself ready, I use that pact to get my mind ready for the day. I run through the list and ask myself, "How am I doing with x, y, and z? What area of my pact should I focus my energy on better embodying today? Are the things I'm pursuing and expending my energy on in alignment with me and my pact?" This pact gives me a moment of mindfulness and self-reflection each day to check in on myself and make sure I'm living in alignment. Here's what a pact might look like:

**The Pact: [insert year] is the Year of Showing Up**

**I will...**

- **consistently show up for myself and my dreams**
- **act in my own best interest**
- **consult God in my endeavors**
- **prioritize fueling my body properly**
- **always appreciate my sublime light**
- **not compare my success to others**
- **let love flow freely from me and to me**
- **prioritize gratitude and meditation**
- **show up in learning mode not performing mode**
- **put forth the effort to create an ambitious tribe around me**
- **be patient with life's timing**
- **take the seat**

**Signature:**

When it comes to goal setting, remember that the physical structure is not without the mental structure. If you want to change your life, it starts with your mind. The "being" is not without the "doing."

# 23

# Dancing with the Waves

I first decided I wanted to write a book in 2016 when I was fifteen. That was when I really started to see and understand the power of storytelling. On April 26, 2019, I sat on a VASA weight bench and came up with the idea for the concept of this book initially titled, "So I'm 18, Now What?" On March 26, 2020, I started writing this book just at the start of the COVID pandemic. Over two years, I intermittently created this story, this journal, this record of who I am and what I've learned. After 7 years since this book writing idea first hit me, I've done a lot of healing, studying, writing, interviewing, speaking, researching, learning, and growing, and I look back and see how this book has truly grown with me over key periods of my life. I will submit this manuscript to my editor this coming Monday and I'm reflecting on the hours of conversations, research, planning, crying, laughing, typing, soul-searching, and undying support from my mom and sister through this endeavor. Thank you, guys. I walk into bookstores now with an amazing amount of gratitude for all the humanity stacked up on those shelves.

At the start of this book-writing journey, in early 2020, I felt very conflicted in pinpointing why I felt this book needed to be written. I realized, it was because I believe in the power of showing our humanity, our humanness. Turning off the smoke and mirrors and showing up as ourselves allows for connection and love. The world needs more connection and love.

On top of that, I believe in your individual sublime power and potential. The fact that the universe is so large and daunting, to me, doesn't mean we are insignificant as individual people. Human connection. Love. Our sublime essence or admirational beauty means something. Maybe that's just what I choose to believe, but I believe you matter. Your light, your vulnerabilities, your love is needed. I don't believe you just happen to be here, or just happened to be reading this book. Your being, your humanness, is needed at this time. I don't know why exactly, but something powerful leads me to believe that to be true. We need you.

I wrote the following piece when I first started the creation of this book that helped direct me to the above conclusion. The conclusion that I believe in the power of the individual's sublime essence and that our collective humanity is so powerful. You are a being of beauty and greatness.

## Dancing with The Waves
## Written 1:22 AM - May 28, 2020

A few years ago, I stood on the beach in San Diego, California. (When I wrote this, I didn't know I'd be living in SD just over a year later, pretty crazy.) The sun warmed the back of my neck and the fresh ocean air filled my lungs. My hands gripped the wooden fence that lined the edge of the beach's cliff as I watched the massive waves roll in and out. I was watching a surfer. The waves moved in beautiful, strong, and powerful breaths before each crashed into the jagged, rocky coast ahead of them. The surfer danced with the waves, fully appreciating their **sublimity**. I watched him willingly and peacefully look into the face of something with such power, the waves, with no fear. It is the power and grandness of the waves that make them so beautiful.

I'm not sure what it is about the wave of big, challenging moments in our lives that tend to stop us in our tracks. Maybe the rush of fear, pain, or anxiety they cause. We let our lens of fear and doubt, created by our lack of faith and hope, cloud our eyes from seizing what is right in front of us. We stop ourselves from opportunity, genuine joy, connection, fulfillment, and love. I can't say yet how to always face life's amazingly, terrifying waves with **courage** and self-compassion. But maybe that's what makes the waves, or the big choices or challenges in our life, so perfect. Our inability to dance with them in perfection. They keep us growing and actualizing our potential.

Not only are life's big moments' powerful like the waves, but so are we.

We are powerful beings worthy of adoration. We can seize the power of life's waves to exalt us into higher greatness. We are beautiful and **powerful**, and we tend to forget or discredit that.

Sometimes we ignore our sublimity for fear if we recognize it, it will crush and drown us if we never actualize it. But there is no prerequisite or earthly state we must reach to be **worthy** of our sublimity. I believe we were each patiently created by an Almighty and All-Powerful being. Our greatness is innate and undeniable.

As we progress through life we learn to work in harmony with our power as we tap deeper and deeper into our greatness, but growth is a scary process. What I've learned is that the trick is to find **equanimity** in the uncertainty of our natural progression. When we understand that life will always be uncertain and make peace with that, that is when we will learn to dance with life's big waves. When we become grateful for the waves of life. We would never have the ability to fully access our power without the moments of beauty and pain the waves provide.

I believe opposition doesn't enter our lives because of some grand design necessarily, contrary to many beliefs. It is just the way life naturally rolls out. We live in a world made of **imperfect** beings and if we were all perfect, what would be the point?

The design of the Universe is made to evolve, the planets are made to be in motion, and we are made to take part in the inevitable motion of time and experience. Through that time and experience, we ourselves get to grow and evolve.

Through the moments of fear and pain life's waves provide, we tap into our vulnerability and self-honesty. Humans are made to feel and if we shut off our valve to fully experience uncomfortable vulnerability, we also shut off our valve to fully experience pure happiness – **joy**.

To feel is to breathe. You need each lung, joy and pain, to survive in abundance. You need emotions that bring you to your knees in **gratitude** and love, as well as confusion and fear. They are not one without the other, as light does not exist without darkness. But darkness gives us the gift to fully appreciate the light.

I thank God for letting me play a role in life's beautifully composed tragedy and to experience the world's incomprehensible rhythm. Let us choose to dance with the waves. Let us recognize our sublime similarities to the ocean's waves, as well.

Let us choose to humbly access our magnificent capacity for love. Love of life. Love of self. Love of tragedy. **Love of humanity**. Let us all choose love. Love is strength. Love is sublime. Love is the sun that keeps our planets in motion and keeps the waves inviting us all to dance.

Keep dancing. I know sometimes it's hard and life gets heavy, but if we can tap into our power, we can find the rhythm again. I feel so grateful that despite the dark times when there felt like there was nothing to keep you dancing, you chose hope. You chose love and resilience.

I believe you're a good person. A good person that holds greatness within. You are a person this world needs. I don't say that lightly, *at all*. I look in the eyes of one individual and I see the universe, I see one more beam of light that helps keep the rest of us dancing.

Remember there is no script; you're not doing life wrong. We're all winging it, all struggling, and as my Nana would say "it's all just a part of the fun." Beauty, failure, confusion, love, and growth lie ahead for us all and I can't wait to see what your intrinsic sublime essence has in store for the world. Lastly, don't forget to laugh at yourself. Life usually isn't as serious as we make it out to be.

I'm rooting for you.

Sincerely Your Friend,

*Livi Redden*

# Acknowledgements

Shoutout to all the amazing, sexy, dope people in my life for helping me give birth to this orange, paperback baby of mine. I freakin love you guys. Jiminy Christmas, where do I begin...

MOM: For loving me as I learned to love myself. Trusting me as I learned to trust myself. Believing in me as I learned to believe in myself. and a million thank yous for your hundreds of hours invested into conversation, listening, and idea bouncing that helped me push this book out of my mental vagina.

LEXI: For comforting me at my lows. Supporting me at my highs. Understanding me when I felt alone. Glad we came out of the same womb homie.

Wow this is really hard, I'll keep the rest of these short and sweet:

DAD for laughing. RACHEL for listening. GREG & LESLEY-ANNE for editing. VANESSA for designing. GOD for loving. ANCESTORS for comforting. UNIVERSE for providing. KODA for hugging. PRISTIQ for existing. MAUREEN & NATALIE for adopting. HOLLY, KRISTEN, & EMI for reviewing. ALLISON for messaging. FAITH & TAYLOR for filming. CLEAR, BRACKETT, SADHGURU, BROWN,

SINCERO, DISPENZA, BOTTON, JAY, & FIELDS for inspiring. BRAD for serving. HUMBLE for believing. PAIGE for watering. BOBBY for marrying. LAUREN for shaping. NANA for relishing. TITF PODCAST GUESTS for collaborating. TIK TOK SUPPORTERS for participating. ALL THE RELATIVES, FRIENDS, NEIGHBORS, MENTORS, COWORKERS, TEACHERS, LEADERS, & COMMUNITIES for supporting. HUMANS for shining.

YOU for reading.

# About the Author

Livi Redden is a mindset educator, author, podcaster, and entrepreneur that guides teens and twentysomethings on how to intentionally steer their life through the power of emotional intelligence, mindfulness, and accountability.

Her social media content surrounding these topics has impacted millions across various platforms. Livi's podcast, Today is the Future, digs into the stories, advice, and mindsets of inspiring, ambitious young adults from all over the world.

Beyond this, Livi is a seeker of adrenaline, taker of dance breaks, lover of fashion, collector of hobbies, and petter of dogs.

**liviredden.com | @liviredden**